MW00461537

"Dave Brunn's study is a breath of . English Bible versions demonstrates that there is more overlap than is often recognized in the translation principles used in different English versions. Translators share common goals of accuracy to the original text and of effective communication, though often with varying focuses and different audiences in mind. Such different perspectives can be an enhancement, facilitating a better understanding of the Biblical text, instead of being a cause of division.

"With numerous convincing examples, Brunn demonstrates that the divide between versions that claim to be 'literal' and those that claim to be 'dynamic' or 'meaning-based' is not as sharp as might appear. The translation of a given verse in a specific 'literal' version may not infrequently be found to be more dynamic than the rendering found in a 'dynamic' version at that point, and vice versa. He also challenges the claim that increased literalness can be equated with increased faithfulness, illustrating extensively how differences in grammar, idioms and lexical correspondence in different languages necessitate adjustments in form if faithful communication is to be achieved. The study is enriched by the author's long experience of translation into a Papua New Guinean language, for people of a totally different culture. He focuses on the realities of translation, not only on theory and principles, combining deep concern for integrity in the translation of Scripture with realistic appreciation of the differences between languages.

"Instead of a spirit of competition and criticism, Brunn advocates appreciating the strengths of different approaches, recognizing the core principles of accuracy and faithfulness that all seek to achieve. He calls for mutual respect and understanding. Concern for faithful communication should draw people together in examining objective evidence. In the past this concern has too often fostered division when those of different opinions take a stand on one issue instead of seeking to study the whole communication picture. This book is a significant contribution to fostering Christian unity in respect of Bible translation through promoting better understanding of the translation process and of the common values that are shared by the translators of different versions."

KATHARINE G. L. BARNWELL, international translation consultant, Summer Institute of Linguistics

"This interesting and important book, written by someone who has devoted many years of his life to Bible translation, is particularly fascinating because it avoids jumping from disputed theory to hard examples. Rather, it jumps from thousands of examples to genuine wisdom on translation issues—along with at least some of the bearing of these examples on theory. This book will diffuse some of the polarizations that characterize many of the disputes. It will also encourage us to recognize we are not as far apart as some of us have supposed, and remind us of how difficult good Bible translation is and how grateful we should be for the wonderful and even complementary choices we have in English Bibles."

D. A. CARSON, Trinity Evangelical Divinity School

"It is a joy to recommend this book to every serious student of the Scriptures. I have read through the whole book carefully; the author has done a tremendous amount of research, looking at passage after passage in many English versions. He has shown clearly, in his text and in his many, many charts, that the versions that are traditionally classified as 'literal' are not as literal as they have been considered to be, and that they are not consistent in their literalness. He has also shown why literal translation is impossible, not only in English, but more so in highly agglutinative languages like the one in which he worked in Papua New Guinea. It is my sincere hope that this book will have an impact on many who think it is a worthwhile endeavor to fight fellow believers over literal translation(s)."

ELLIS W. DEIBLER JR., international translation consultant, Wycliffe Bible Translators

"*One Bible, Many Versions* is very well written. It is, in fact, one of the finest treatments of the subject of translation that I have been privileged to read. In the providence of God I trust that many, many others will read this book and benefit from it as I have."

DAVID J. HESSELGRAVE, Trinity Evangelical Divinity School

"Dave Brunn's book does a wonderful job of showing that even those translations that are promoted as 'literal' or 'essentially literal' often provide interpretive renderings of the original texts, and that this is not a bad thing but part of what one should expect in any translation. This valuable book demonstrates that the distinctive claims often made for translations— namely that they are literal and do not engage in interpretive renderings like other translations—have more to do with rhetoric than with reality, and reinforce unhelpful misconceptions about what translation actually entails. I highly recommend it!"

ROY E. CIAMPA, Gordon-Conwell Theological Seminary

"*One Bible, Many Versions* is a careful study of various translations from someone who has wrestled with translation. It shows that claims of literal and otherwise are not always what they seem in part because of the difficulty of doing translation work well for those in the receiving language and the options translators face in translating. If you want to understand translation work and appreciate what English translations do and how, then this book is for you. I think you will find the study illuminating."

DARRELL L. BOCK, Dallas Theological Seminary

"While we have technical resources on linguistics and translation theory, *One Bible, Many Versions* pans the research and rancor for valuable insights. Dave Brunn's work is refreshing because it focuses on the translation evidence, marks the progress and subtly calls all parties to civil dialogue."

ANDREW J. SCHMUTZER, Moody Bible Institute

"Bible teachers at every level will find this book an invaluable source of practical illustrations, charts, graphs and clear thinking regarding the process of transferring the message of the Bible from its original languages to modern ones. The book should be required reading for every serious Bible student."

GAYLEN LEVERETT, Liberty University

"In this book Dave Brunn raises the important and fascinating question, how literal should a Bible translation be? As there is no universal agreement on the answer to this question and as the issue is of considerable importance his work is timely and should prove helpful to pastors, translators and all who seek to 'rightly handle the Word of God.'"

STUART BRISCOE, minister-at-large, Elmbrook Church

"The gospel was originally spoken to us in the historically conditioned forms of the Hebrew, Aramaic and Greek languages of antiquity, and the Lord commanded us to pass that gospel on to *all* nations until the end of the age. Faithful and reliable translations of those Scriptures are the essence of obedience to that commandment. And what a task it is! Translation is the responsibility of the entire church even if in particular ways it is the labor of specialized professionals. Ultimately the work of translating the Bible into English, to limit ourselves to this one language, requires knowledge across a range of fields, among which are translation theory, the original languages of Scripture, the English language, linguistics, exegesis and theology, and the history, aims and users of previous and existing English translations— not to mention a stance of faithfulness from within the life of that very gospel. It is to be expected that so great a task would strain our best minds, and it is understandable if it should occasion principled disagreement. For the nonspecialist some of this disagreement is bound to breed uncertainty. Understanding and confidence are what we seek. What is therefore to be hoped is that a voice such as Dave Brunn's will be heard, combining as it does theoretical and practical knowledge with a spirit of charity, peace and faithful devotion. Among his credentials, Brunn spent two decades translating the Scriptures into a language outside the Indo-European family to which English belongs, affording him invaluable comparative perspective. To this he adds the graces of a gifted teacher: clarity, patience, humility and remarkable empathy for readers who have little or no experience in the languages and other challenges of translation. Easy-to-understand charts and illustrations abound. Moreover, his aims are not bound up with any particular translation but with the interests of the church and the gospel. Without presuming to have written the final word, Brunn has written a good book and modeled for us how to have a conversation."

JON LAANSMA, Wheaton College and Graduate School

ONE BIBLE,
MANY VERSIONS

Are All Translations Created Equal?

◆ ◆ ◆

DAVE BRUNN

IVP Academic

An imprint of InterVarsity Press
Downers Grove, Illinois

Inter-Varsity Press

Nottingham, England

InterVarsity Press, USA
P.O. Box 1400
Downers Grove, IL 60515-1426, USA
World Wide Web: www.ivpress.com
Email: email@ivpress.com

Inter-Varsity Press, England
Norton Street
Nottingham NG7 3HR, England
Website: www.ivpbooks.com
Email: ivp@ivpbooks.com

InterVarsity Press® is the book-publishing division of InterVarsity Christian Fellowship/USA®, a movement of students and faculty active on campus at hundreds of universities, colleges and schools of nursing in the United States of America, and a member movement of the International Fellowship of Evangelical Students. For information about local and regional activities, write Public Relations Dept., InterVarsity Christian Fellowship/USA, 6400 Schroeder Rd., P.O. Box 7895, Madison, WI 53707-7895, or visit the IVCF website at <www.intervarsity.org>.

Inter-Varsity Press, England, is closely linked with the Universities and Colleges Christian Fellowship, a student movement connecting Christian Unions throughout Great Britain, and a member movement of the International Fellowship of Evangelical Students. Website: www.uccf.org.uk

Design: Cindy Kiple
Images: Photo of books: David Fassett
      Open Bible: © DNY59/iStockphoto
Interior design: Beth Hagenberg

US ISBN 978-0-8308-2715-2
UK ISBN 978-1-84474-625-5

Printed in the United States of America ∞

Library of Congress Cataloging-in-Publication Data

Brunn, Dave, 1955-
  One Bible, many versions : are all translations created equal? / Dave Brunn.
    pages cm
  Includes bibliographical references and index.
  ISBN 978-0-8308-2715-2 (pbk. : alk. paper)
  1. Bible. English—Versions. 2. Bible—Translating. I. Title.
  BS455.B78 2013
  220.4—dc23

                                              2012045945

British Library Cataloguing in Publication Data

A catalogue record for this book is available from the British Library.

P	21	20	19	18	17	16	15	14	13	12	11	10	9	8	7	6	5	4	3	2	1
Y	31	30	29	28	27	26	25	24	23	22	21	20	19	18	17	16	15	14	13

To the unity of the body of Christ,

for the glory of God,

through his eternal Word

CONTENTS

ACKNOWLEDGMENTS

◆ ◆ ◆

I am indebted to the following individuals for their kind support of this project and their insightful input: Greg Melendes, Mark Strauss, D. A. Carson, David Hesselgrave, Ruth Brendle, James D. Smith III, Ron Van Peursem, Ric Bruce III, Ellis Deibler, Dick Kroneman, Brandon Flint, Bill Davis, Jim Weaver, Tom Steffen, Brendan Kennedy, Gary Gilley, George Hertwig, Katy Barnwell, Larry Brown, John Brennan and Valdecio da Silva.

I would also like to thank Gary Deddo and David Congdon, my Inter-Varsity Press editors, and the rest of the fine people at IVP for believing in this project and for using their expertise to enhance the quality of the finished product.

I am grateful to my earliest teachers and mentors in the field of Bible translation: Bob Gustafson, Jean Johnson, Jerry Fitzgerald, Carol Kaptain, Dan Shaw and Jacob Loewen.

Additionally, I am grateful to my Lamogai co-translators in Papua New Guinea, especially Kapakio, Ros, Monsen and Sadidok, for their commitment to the translation task and for their role in helping me learn many invaluable lessons about Bible translation.

I am also grateful to my missionary colleagues in the Lamogai church-planting effort—Mike and Sandy Mikolavich, Kevin and Marge Jenson, Jan and Annette Wols, Dave and Patti Hodgdon, and Rory and Mary Fuller—for their part in establishing strong, indigenous Lamogai churches, including comprehensive, ongoing Bible teaching programs in the Lamogai language, which assure that the published Lamogai Scriptures will continue to be read and studied on a regular basis by many Lamogai Christians.

I must also thank the hundreds of students who sat in my Bible translation classes over the past decade. They asked a lot of hard questions that forced me to hone my message and refine my illustrative examples.

I am grateful for the godly example of my parents and their influence on my life and ministry, even now as they enjoy their third decade of retirement and their seventh decade of marriage.

I am also grateful to Pastor Von (E. G. Von Trutzschler),[1] my former youth pastor, now an octogenarian. God used him in a powerful way to steer me toward a ministry of Bible translation and church planting among unreached people groups. Pastor Von relentlessly challenged us as young people to invest our lives for eternity, and he backed up his words with a life of true sacrifice.

It gives me great pleasure to thank my life partner and soul mate, Nancy—the wife of my youth, the mother of my children and the grandmother of my grandchildren—for her love and patience and for the support she gives in more ways than I can count.

Above all, I am grateful to my Lord and Savior Jesus Christ for allowing me to serve him through translation, teaching and writing. In his providence and by his grace, I trust that my modest efforts will be an anthem of worship to his name. May I continually walk close to him and serve him faithfully until the day I see his face.

---

[1]www.pastorvon.com.

PREFACE

◆◆◆

The year was 1989. It was a typical hot, steamy afternoon in the little jungle village in Papua New Guinea that we had learned to call home. I was sitting alone in my undersized office, wrapping up another long day of translating the Bible[1] into the language of the Lamogai (*lah-moh-guy*) people.[2] My Lamogai co-translators had left for the day. As I reflected on the verses we had just finished, I felt a deep sense of satisfaction in being able to translate the Scriptures for this forgotten group of people. At the same time, I felt a huge weight of responsibility knowing I would someday hand them a completed New Testament and tell them, "This is God's Word."

By God's grace, I pressed forward in faith with the Lamogai translation. It was very much a joint venture. As the missionary-translator, my primary focus was exegesis—making sure we correctly understood the meaning of the Scripture passages we were translating. My cherished Lamogai co-translators were the experts in the target language—their own, of course. Every word of the first draft of the translation came out of their mouths, not mine.

Throughout the entire process, there was a multilayered partnership at work: collaboration between the missionary and the mother-tongue speakers, communion between the Holy Spirit and the translation team as a whole and correlation between the form of the message and the meaning of the

---

[1]The body of published Scripture in the Lamogai language includes the entire New Testament along with key Old Testament portions. Most of the Old Testament portions were translated by another member of our team.

[2]The Lamogai people live in West New Britain Province (on New Britain Island), Papua New Guinea.

message. Mutual participation was essential on every level of partnership.

As the translation moved forward, our missionary team was able to teach the Lamogai people the timeless truths of God's Word in their own language. We laid a foundation starting with the book of Genesis, chronologically teaching key portions from the Old Testament and the life of Christ to give them an understanding of the full meaning of the gospel message.[3] But the initial response was minimal, particularly among the adult men of the village. At one point, we asked ourselves, "Will there be any Lamogai believers serious enough about their faith to partner with us in taking the gospel to the rest of the Lamogai villages?"

By the time the Lamogai New Testament[4] was published in 1996, however, God had done an amazing work in their hearts. Many of the villagers, including several of the key patriarchal leaders, had placed their trust in the Lord Jesus Christ as their personal Savior. God continually reminded us that it was not about us or our efforts. We made the living truths of God's Word available to the Lamogai people. Only God could change their hearts.

I look back with fond memories on the years I spent doing Bible translation. What an awesome privilege it was to spend several hours each day digging into the eternal truths of the inspired Scriptures. What a privilege to see those truths transform the lives of my dear Lamogai friends—now my brothers and sisters in Christ. And what a privilege it was to be part of a team that experienced the deep sense of unity that springs from a common commitment to God's truth.

---

[3]Our approach to evangelism and church planting among the Lamogai people was largely based on the principles and Bible teaching outlines contained in the series Building on Firm Foundations, vols. 1-9, by Trevor McIlwain, published by New Tribes Mission, Sanford, FL (www.ntm.org).

[4]*Panggo ilo Kanesngen ka Testamen Tangan Ino* (The New Testament published for the people of the Lamogai and Paret areas of Papua New Guinea) (Sanford, FL: New Tribes Mission, 1996).

ABBREVIATIONS

English Bible Versions

AMP	Amplified Bible
ASV	American Standard Version
CEV	Contemporary English Version
ESV	English Standard Version
GW	God's Word
HCSB	Holman Christian Standard Bible
KJV	King James Version
MESSAGE	The Message
NASB	New American Standard Bible
NCV	New Century Version
NET	New English Translation (NET Bible)
NIV	New International Version
NRSV	New Revised Standard Version
PHILLIPS	Phillips New Testament in Modern English
RSV	Revised Standard Version
TEV	Today's English Version
TYNDALE	Tyndale Translation
VOICE	The Voice Bible
WYCLIFFE	Wycliffe Translation
YLT	Young's Literal Translation

Other Abbreviations

BHS	Biblica Hebraica Stuttgartiensia
CT	Critical Text
Gk	Greek
Heb	Hebrew
lit	literal, literally
LXX	Septuagint
TR	Textus Receptus

INTRODUCTION

◆◆◆

More than thirty years ago, when I was preparing for missionary service, I read a powerful book on Bible translation that was hot off the press: D. A. Carson's *The King James Version Debate: A Plea for Realism.*[1] In the years since that time, another growing view of translation has emerged within evangelical Christianity: the literal-only or literal-superiority position. There is no doubt in my mind that those who hold these points of view are driven by a firm commitment to guarding the faithfulness and accuracy of God's Word. Problems arise, however, when the issue of translation theory, on which the Bible is virtually silent, is elevated to the level of doctrine.

The underlying translation principles that Dr. Carson skillfully wove into his book thirty years ago still ring true, and they pertain in a real sense to the current discussion surrounding the literal-only or literal-superiority view. For me, those elemental principles were like seeds that took root and grew into a perspective on translation which serves as the starting point for much of what I have written in this book. Now it is my turn to offer another "plea for realism."

CHAPTER-BY-CHAPTER SYNOPSIS

In the preface to the book and in chapter one, I give a brief sketch of my years as a missionary-translator, explaining the dilemma I faced trying to determine what it means to translate the Scriptures "faithfully" and "accu-

---

[1]D. A. Carson, *The King James Version Debate: A Plea for Realism* (Grand Rapids: Baker Book House, 1979).

rately." This dilemma became even more complex when I began to realize that every "literal" version frequently sets aside its own standards of literalness and word-for-word translation.

Chapter two outlines the relationship between the form of the message and the meaning of the message. A major focus of this chapter is idioms and figures of speech, since that is one of the easiest places to start developing a correct understanding of form and meaning in translation.

Chapter three highlights the importance of focusing not only on translation ideals but also on the real world of translation practice. When the translation debate is confined to the realm of philosophical ideals, it often comes down to little more than a difference of opinion.

Chapter four concentrates on the translation of the words of Scripture, since that is a major focal point of the literal translation debate.

Chapter five explains four basic reasons why translators of every English version, including the most literal ones, have frequently set aside the standard of literal, word-for-word translation.

Chapter six explores the relationship between the doctrine of inspiration and the practice of translation: Does a truly biblical doctrine of inspiration require all translators to embrace only certain translation ideals? There are many compelling examples in this chapter supporting the premise that literal Bible versions in English are not nearly as literal as many Christians perceive them to be.

Chapter seven demonstrates that the challenge of trying to achieve word-for-word translation escalates sharply when we move from English to languages outside of the Indo-European family. One reason we are able to achieve the level of literalness that exists in some English versions (especially of the New Testament) is that English and Greek are both Indo-European languages.

Chapter eight provides evidence that even the human authors of the New Testament did not always aim for word-for-word equivalence when they quoted or translated Old Testament verses.

Chapter nine draws a parallel between the current translation debate and a similar debate that took place in the nineteenth century, initiated by Robert Young, translator of *Young's Literal Translation*. This chapter also discusses the injection of interpretation into the translation of Scripture.

Chapter ten summarizes the book, reviewing from earlier chapters a number of key features that all English Bible versions have in common. This chapter also underscores the fact that God's principle of interdependence is at the heart of true unity.

As you read this book you will find that it includes a significant number of examples, charts and illustrative diagrams. My intention in this is to let the real evidence speak for itself rather than arguing theoretical ideals.

There are also many explanatory footnotes throughout the book. Most of these footnotes are intended to answer questions that would likely be raised by readers who are already knowledgeable in translation issues.

Toward a Deeper Sense of Unity

It is not my aim in writing this book to add fuel to the ongoing translation debate. On the contrary, I trust that the need for this debate will diminish as we explore key spheres of evidence that have often been left out of the discussion.

Rather than emphasizing the differences between Bible versions, I will highlight the similarities. Rather than making a case for one philosophical position, I hope to bring the philosophical positions closer together. Rather than describing dissimilar Bible versions as mutually contradictory, I aim to demonstrate that they are often mutually complementary—even mutually dependent.

It is my heartfelt prayer that this book will make some small contribution toward promoting the kind of unity God intends his Word to foster among his children.

1

Unity and Division

Two Opposite Byproducts of God's Word

◆ ◆ ◆

So we, being many, are one body in Christ,
and every one members one of another.

Romans 12:5 (kjv)

For the word of God is living and powerful,
and sharper than any two-edged sword,
piercing even to the division of soul and spirit,
and of joints and marrow, and is a discerner
of the thoughts and intents of the heart.

Hebrews 4:12 (nkjv)

Down through the ages, the Bible has been a vital source of unity among Christians. At the same time, it has been an important instrument of separation, maintaining a boundary between truth and falsehood, between genuine believers and unbelievers.

In modern times, particularly in recent decades, the Bible has become the focal point of a new kind of division. This division does not separate believers and unbelievers but believers from other believers. It is not a division based on theology or the interpretation of any biblical doctrine. Instead, it is a line of demarcation that focuses on differing standards for translating God's Word, particularly as it is translated into English.

There are several debates within Christianity about Bible translation. For instance, some Christians believe there is only one authentic English version. Others accept only one Greek textual tradition. These are not the issues I will address here. In this book, I will examine the question of literalness in translation: How literal should a Bible translation be? Are literal versions the only valid versions?

IN SEARCH OF THE RIGHT STANDARDS

There are many Bible translations available in the English language, each unique in a number of ways. Most of the differences between these versions can be traced to the standards of translation employed by the translators. While all translators agree that there must be standards for Bible translation, the point of disagreement centers on what those standards should be. At the heart of this discussion are these kinds of questions:

- What makes a translation of the Scriptures faithful and accurate?
- Should all translators aim to reach word-for-word equivalence with the original?
- Are meaning-based (or dynamic equivalence[1]) translations legitimate?
- What is the significance of the original form and the original meaning?

These questions about translation are very different from questions of doctrine. Doctrinal questions can be answered by searching the Scriptures. But the Bible does not give instructions on how to translate a written message from one language to another. Without the testimony of Scripture, how can we know for sure which translation standards are the right ones?

---

[1]In some circles, the term "dynamic equivalence" has been replaced by the updated term "functional equivalence." The reason I have chosen to use the older term "dynamic equivalence" is that some Bible versions, including the ESV and the NASB, still use this term in their prefaces and introductions to describe the strategy employed by translators of nonliteral versions of the Bible. For a brief explanation of the origin of these two terms, see Gordon D. Fee and Mark L. Strauss, *How to Choose a Translation for All Its Worth* (Grand Rapids: Zondervan, 2007), p. 26.

It is imperative that we set and keep standards that will produce faithful translations. At the same time, we need to protect our Christian unity. Jesus' prayer in John 17 seems to draw a connection between God's Word and true unity: "I have given them Your word. . . . Sanctify them in the truth; Your word is truth. . . . [I pray] that they may all be one . . . so that the world may believe that You sent Me" (Jn 17:14-21 NASB). Obviously, Jesus was not suggesting that we compromise truth for the sake of so-called unity. That would be false unity. Commenting on this prayer of Jesus, John MacArthur writes, "The unity Jesus prayed for is a unity based on common commitment to truth. It is a oneness made possible because we are sanctified in the truth, not a false unity borne of compromise."[2]

We cannot allow false unity to dilute the purity of God's Word, nor can we allow differing viewpoints to divide us unnecessarily. If we are willing to allow our convictions about translation standards to cause disagreement among us, we need to be certain that those standards are built on a rock-solid foundation. In this book, we will examine some of the underlying reasons for this ongoing debate, and in the end, I believe we will discover the chasm between the different schools of thought is not as wide as it is often perceived to be.

Leading advocates on both sides of this issue are godly men and women who possess the "common commitment to truth" that MacArthur wrote about. Both sides hold to a steadfast belief in one eternal, triune God. Both sides believe in Christ's deity, his virgin birth, sinless life, atoning death and bodily resurrection. Both sides affirm the gospel of salvation by grace through faith alone and zealously defend the divine inspiration of Scripture. Thus, the issues surrounding the translation of God's written Word have become the focal point of a disagreement between Christians who are like-minded in the most essential truths addressed therein.

I do not want to overstate the issue at hand. I am not suggesting that this is the most dangerous of all disagreements facing Christianity today. Yet the Bible makes it clear that every potential source of disunity among Christians can be dangerous (1 Cor 1–4). Unwarranted division harms the church and inevitably reduces its effectiveness in reaching out to a lost world.

---

[2]John MacArthur Jr., *Deadly Trends of Popular Christianity* (Panorama City, CA: Grace to You, 1990).

THE POWERFUL EFFECT OF GOD'S WORD

As a young Christian in the early 1970s, I discovered the realm of meaningful Bible exposition as it was opened up to me by my teachers and mentors at Bible school[3]—and through outstanding Bible teachers on the radio.[4] I sent away for cassette tapes of their teaching and feasted on the deep spiritual insights they offered. The more I learned, the more I found myself drawn to a full-time ministry focused on God's Word.

The Lord used this growing love for his Word coupled with a keen interest in linguistics to lead me to a ministry of overseas missionary service. It was a dream come true for an enthusiastic, young student of the Bible like me. In the years to follow, I had the privilege of translating God's Word and teaching it (as part of a team) to a remote people group who had never had access to the Scriptures in their own language—the Lamogai (*lah-moh-guy*) people of Papua New Guinea (PNG).

Meanwhile, a world away, controversy regarding translation principles was brewing. It continued to escalate during the twenty-one years that my wife, Nancy, and I served as missionaries in PNG (1980–2001). Fortunately, this debate never made its way to the secluded jungle villages where the Lamogai people live because it would have been mostly irrelevant to them anyway. I found that some of the widely accepted litmus tests of faithful and accurate translation at the heart of this debate were based on English grammatical features that are nonexistent in the Lamogai language. This realization evoked a recurring, unshakable question in my mind: If the Lamogai language by its nature fails some of the recognized tests of faithful translation, is it legitimate to apply those tests in a strict fashion to every English Bible version? At the same time, as I spent months and years working through the translation process, I had the privilege of examining the Scriptures in ways I never had before. This deeper examination led me to conclude that the seemingly literal versions of the Bible in English are not nearly as literal as I had previously thought.

"WORD FOR WORD" OR "THOUGHT FOR THOUGHT"?

Every time I approached a passage of Scripture to translate it into Lamogai,

---

[3]New Tribes Bible Institute (www.ntm.org/ntbi).
[4]"Grace to You" with John MacArthur (www.gty.org); "Thru the Bible Radio" with J. Vernon McGee (www.thruthebible.org).

I studied the original wording and compared it with several English Bible versions. When I did, I found a few surprises. Of course, some versions translated the original words literally, while others translated thought for thought—expressing the same basic meaning in different words. For example, in Jeremiah 48:45 (see table 1.1), the New King James Version (NKJV) and the English Standard Version (ESV) translated the phrase "sons of tumult" literally, but another version rephrased it as "riotous revelers." And in 2 Timothy 2:5 (table 1.2), the NKJV and ESV gave a word-for-word translation of the phrase "is not crowned," but another version translated it thought for thought as "does not win the prize."

Table 1.1

Jeremiah 48:45		
	Hebrew	*sons of tumult*
Literal	NKJV	sons of tumult
	ESV	sons of tumult
Thought for Thought		riotous revelers

Table 1.2

2 Timothy 2:5		
	Greek	*is not crowned*
Literal	NKJV	is not crowned
	ESV	is not crowned
Thought for Thought		does not win the prize

It is no surprise that literal versions like the NKJV and ESV translated these phrases word for word. But you may be surprised, as I was, to find the version that translated thought for thought in these two examples is the New American Standard Bible (NASB)—which describes itself as "the most literal."[5] I consider the NASB to be an excellent translation, and while the thought-for-thought renderings "riotous revelers" and "does not win the prize" are acceptable, they are not literal.[6]

As I pressed forward with the Lamogai translation, I discovered that this sort of thing happens all the time. So I started compiling a list of verses

---

[5]Updated NASB (1995), title page.
[6]The NASB footnote for Jer 48:45 says, "Lit *sons of tumult*," and for 2 Tim 2:5, "Lit *is not crowned*."

where literal versions chose to translate thought for thought rather than
word for word. In table 1.3, I have listed a number of places where the NASB
rephrased part of the meaning in different words even though some other
versions translated it quite literally. As you browse through these examples,
it will become clear beyond doubt that this is a pattern, not a rare phenomenon. Keep in mind that this chart is nowhere near exhaustive; it represents only a fraction of the examples I have found.

Table 1.3

	Essentially Literal Rendering[a]					Thought for Thought
Original Wording[b]	Various Versions					NASB
Gen 4:1	(Adam) knew (Eve)	NKJV	Knew	ESV	Knew	Had relations with
Gen 30:27	If I have found favor in your eyes	NIV	If I have found favor in your eyes	KJV	If I have found favour in thine eyes	If now it pleases you
1 Sam 27:1	David said in his heart	ESV	David said in his heart	NKJV	David said in his heart	David said to himself[c]
2 Chron 15:7	Do not let your hands drop	ESV	Do not let your hands be weak	NKJV	Do not let your hands be weak	Do not lose courage[d]
Job 7:17	That you set your heart on him	ESV	That you set your heart on him	NKJV	That you should set your heart on him	That you are concerned about him
Job 16:9	Sharpens his eyes to me	ESV	Sharpens his eyes against me	NKJV	Sharpens his gaze on me	Glares at me
Job 18:20	Appalled at his day	ESV	Appalled at his day	NKJV	Astonished at his day	Appalled at his fate
Job 27:3	While breath is still in me	HCSB	As long as my breath is still in me	ESV	As long as my breath is in me	As long as life is in me
Job 27:7	He who rises up against me	ESV	Him who rises up against me	NKJV	He who rises up against me	My opponent

[a] I described these renderings as literal because that is how the NASB and other literal versions generally
describe them in their own footnotes. For example, the NASB footnote for Gen 4:1 says, "Lit *knew*."
[b] The original wording for most of these examples is based on footnotes in the NASB.
[c] In this chart (table 1.3), the NASB did not provide a literal translation of the word *heart* in 1 Sam 27:1; Job 7:17;
Eccles 7:21; Ezek 13:2; Dan 7:28. See Wayne Grudem, "Are Only *Some* Words of Scripture Breathed Out by
God? Why Plenary Inspiration Favors 'Essentially Literal' Bible Translation," in C. John Collins, Wayne Gru-
dem, Vern Sheridan Poythress, Leland Ryken and Bruce Winter, *Translating Truth: The Case for Essentially
Literal Bible Translation* (Wheaton, IL: Crossway, 2005), pp. 44-45, under the heading "The Missing Heart."
[d] In this chart (table 1.3), the NASB did not provide a literal translation of the word *hand(s)* in 2 Chron 15:7;
Eccles 5:14; Jer 38:4; 46:24; Lam 5:6; Zech 11:6; Mt 26:51; Acts 7:25, 35; 11:30. See Grudem, "Are Only *Some*
Words of Scripture Breathed Out by God?" pp. 35-37, under the heading "The Missing Hands."

		Essentially Literal Rendering[a]			Thought for Thought
Original Wording[b]		Various Versions			NASB
Job 31:18	*From my mother's womb*	ESV	From my mother's womb	NKJV	From my mother's womb	From infancy
Job 31:27	*My hand kissed my mouth*	ESV	My mouth has kissed my hand	NKJV	My mouth has kissed my hand	My hand threw a kiss from my mouth
Ps 2:9	*Potter's vessel*	ESV	Potter's vessel	NKJV	Potter's vessel	Earthenware
Ps 35:15	*They tore [me]*	HCSB	They . . . tore at me	ESV	They . . . tore at me	They slandered me
Ps 146:3	*A son of man*	ESV	A son of man	NKJV	A son of man	Mortal man
Prov 12:14	*Fruit of his mouth*	ESV	Fruit of his mouth	NKJV	Fruit of his mouth	Fruit of his words
Eccles 5:14	*Nothing in his hand*	ESV	Nothing in his hand	NKJV	Nothing in his hand	Nothing to support him
Eccles 7:21	*Do not give your heart to*	ESV	Do not take to heart	NKJV	Do not take to heart	Do not take seriously
Eccles 8:12	*Fear before him*	ESV	Fear before him	NKJV	Fear before him	Fear Him openly
Eccles 10:13	*The words of his mouth*	HCSB	The words of his mouth	ESV	The words of his mouth	His talking
Eccles 11:9	*The sights of your eyes*	HCSB	The sights of your eyes	ESV	The sight of your eyes	The desires of your eyes
Song 4:15	*Living water*	ESV	Living water	NKJV	Living waters	Fresh water
Song 8:12	*Before me*	ESV	Before me	NKJV	Before me	At my disposal
Is 1:1	*In the days of Uzziah*	ESV	In the days of Uzziah	NKJV	In the days of Uzziah	During the reigns of Uzziah
Is 8:10	*Speak a word*	ESV	Speak a word	NKJV	Speak the word	State a proposal
Is 9:4	*The day of Midian*	HCSB	The day of Midian	ESV	The day of Midian	The battle of Midian
Is 10:7	*Nations not a few*	ESV	Nations not a few	NKJV	Not a few nations	Many nations
Is 14:30	*The firstborn of the poor (helpless)*	HCSB	The firstborn of the poor	ESV	The firstborn of the poor	Those who are most helpless
Is 30:10	*Smooth things*	ESV	Smooth things	NKJV	Smooth things	Pleasant words

		Essentially Literal Rendering[a]				Thought for Thought
Original Wording[b]		Various Versions				NASB
Is 54:17	*Every tongue that rises against you*	ESV	Every tongue that rises against you	NKJV	Every tongue that rises against you	Every tongue that accuses you
Is 57:19	*Fruit of the lips*	ESV	Fruit of the lips	NKJV	Fruit of the lips	Praise of the lips
Jer 6:10	*Their ears are uncircumcized*	ESV	Their ears are uncircumcized	NKJV	Their ears are uncircumcized	Their ears are closed
Jer 15:19	*You shall become as my mouth*	ESV	You shall be as my mouth	NKJV	You shall be as My mouth	You will become My spokesman
Jer 17:10[e]	*The fruit of his deeds*	ESV	The fruit of his deeds	NKJV	The fruit of his doings	The results of his deeds
Jer 38:4	*Weakening the hands*	ESV	Weakening the hands	NKJV	Weakens the hands	Discouraging
Jer. 42:15[f]	*Set your face*	ESV	Set your faces	NKJV	Set your faces	Set your mind[g]
Jer 46:24[h]	*The hand of the people*	NIV	The hands of the people	NKJV	The hand of the people	The power of the people
Jer 48:45	*Sons of tumult*	ESV	Sons of tumult	NKJV	Sons of tumult	Riotous revelers
Lam 5:6	*Given the hand to Egypt*	ESV	Given the hand to Egypt	NKJV	Given our hand to the Egyptians	Submitted to Egypt
Ezek 3:10	*Listen (hear) with your ears*	ESV	Hear with your ears	NKJV	Hear with your ears	Listen closely
Ezek 12:27	*Many days*	ESV	Many days	NKJV	Many days	Many years
Ezek 13:2[i]	*Their own heart*	ESV	Their own hearts	NKJV	Their own heart	Their own inspiration
Ezek 17:16	*Made him king*	ESV	Made him king	NKJV	Made him king	Put him on the throne
Dan 7:28	*I kept the matter in my heart*	ESV	I kept the matter in my heart	NKJV	I kept the matter in my heart	I kept the matter to myself
Dan 9:3	*I set my face to the Lord God*	ESV	I turned my face to the Lord God	NKJV	I set my face toward the Lord God	I gave my attention to the Lord God

[e] Also Jer 21:14.

[f] Also Jer 42:17; 44:12.

[g] In this chart (table 1.3), the NASB did not provide a literal translation of the word *face(s)* in Jer 42:15; Dan 9:3; Mt 11:10; Lk 9:51. See Grudem, "Are Only *Some* Words of Scripture Breathed Out by God?" pp. 41-42, under the heading "The Lost Faces."

[h] Also Jer 46:26.

[i] Also Ezek 13:17.

			Essentially Literal Rendering[a]				Thought for Thought
Original Wording[b]		Various Versions					NASB
Dan 11:7	*A branch of her roots*	ESV	A branch from her roots	NKJV	A branch of her roots		One of the descendants of her line
Mic 7:5	*Guard the doors of your mouth*	ESV	Guard the doors of your mouth	NKJV	Guard the doors of your mouth		Guard your lips
Hab 1:4	*Justice never goes forth*	ESV	Justice never goes forth	NKJV	Justice never goes forth		Justice is never upheld
Hab 2:16	*Show yourself uncircumcised*	HCSB	Expose your uncircumcision	ESV	Show your uncircumcision		Expose your own nakedness
Zeph 2:14	*A voice*	ESV	A voice	NKJV	Their voice		Birds
Zech 8:17	*False oath*	ESV	False oath	NKJV	False oath		Perjury
Zech 11:6	*The hand of his king*	NIV	The hands of . . . their king	ESV	The hand of his king		The power of his king
Zech 12:4	*I will open my eyes*	ESV	I will keep my eyes open	NKJV	I will open my eyes		I will watch over
Mt 1:25	*Was not knowing her*	HCSB	Did not know her intimately	ESV	Knew her not		Kept her a virgin
Mt 4:7[j]	*Again*	ESV	Again	NKJV	Again		On the other hand
Mt 11:10[k]	*Before your face*	ESV	Before your face	NKJV	Before your face		Ahead of you
Mt 12:16[l]	*Make him known*	HCSB	Make him known	ESV	Make him known		Tell who He was
Mt 24:43[m]	*Know this*	HCSB	Know this	ESV	Know this		Be sure of this
Mt 26:51	*Extended the hand*	HCSB	Reached out his hand	ESV	Stretched out his hand		Reached
Mk 4:30	*To what should we compare the Kingdom of God?*	ESV	With what can we compare the Kingdom of God?	NKJV	To what shall we liken the Kingdom of God?		How shall we picture the Kingdom of God?
Mk 5:28	*She was saying*	HCSB	She said	ESV	She said		She thought
Mk 14:52	*He left behind the linen cloth*	HCSB	He left the linen cloth	ESV	He left the linen cloth		He pulled free of the linen sheet

[j] Also Lk 6:43.
[k] Also Mk 1:2; Lk 7:27.
[l] Also Mk 3:12.
[m] Also Lk 12:39; Gal 3:7.

Original Wording[b]			Essentially Literal Rendering[a] Various Versions			Thought for Thought NASB
Lk 1:13	*Call his name John*	ESV	Call his name John	NKJV	Call his name John	Give him the name John
Lk 1:27	*The house of David*	HCSB	The house of David	ESV	The house of David	The descendants of David
Lk 1:39[n]	*In these days*	HCSB	In those days	ESV	In those days	At this time
Lk 2:36	*From her virginity*	ESV	From when she was a virgin	NKJV	From her virginity	After her marriage
Lk 4:33	*Having a spirit of a demon*	ESV	Had the spirit of [a] . . . demon	NKJV	Had the spirit of a . . . demon	Possessed by the spirit of a . . . demon
Lk 5:5	*Upon your word I will let down the nets*	HCSB	At Your word I will let down the nets	ESV	At your word I will let down the nets	I will do as You say and let down the nets
Lk 6:8	*Their thoughts*	HCSB	Their thoughts	ESV	Their thoughts	What they were thinking
Lk 9:51	*He set his face to go to Jerusalem*	ESV	He set his face to go to Jerusalem	NKJV	He . . . set his face to go to Jerusalem	He was determined to go to Jerusalem
Lk 10:6	*A son of peace*	HCSB	A son of peace	ESV	A son of peace	A man of peace
Lk 10:40	*Much service*	ESV	Much serving	NKJV	Much serving	All her preparations
Lk 12:45	*My master is delaying to come*	HCSB	My master is delaying his coming	ESV	My master is delayed in coming	My master will be a long time in coming
Lk 15:17	*When he came to himself*	ESV	When he came to himself	NKJV	When he came to himself	When he came to his senses
Lk 15:18	*Before you*	ESV	Before you	NKJV	Before you	In your sight
Lk 16:15	*Before men*	ESV	Before men	NKJV	Before men	In the sight of men
Lk 20:33	*Seven had her as wife*	ESV	Seven had her as wife	NKJV	Seven had her as wife	Seven had married her
Lk 21:15	*I will give you a mouth*	ESV	I will give you a mouth	NKJV	I will give you a mouth	I will give you utterance
Acts 7:25	*Through (by) his hand*	ESV	By his hand	NKJV	By his hand	Through him

[n]Also Acts 7:41; 9:37; 11:27.

		Essentially Literal Rendering[a]			Thought for Thought
Original Wording[b]		Various Versions			NASB
Acts 7:35	*The hand of the angel*	ESV	The hand of the angel	NKJV	The hand of the Angel	The help of the angel
Acts 9:28	*With them going in and going out*	ESV	Went in and out among them	NKJV	With them, . . . coming in and going out	With them, moving about freely
Acts 11:30	*By the hand of Barnabas and Saul*	ESV	By the hand of Barnabas and Saul	NKJV	By the hands of Barnabas and Saul	In charge of Barnabas and Saul
Acts 15:2	*No small dissension*	ESV	No small dissension	NKJV	No small dissension	Great dissension
Acts 20:12	*Not moderately comforted*	ESV	Not a little comforted	NKJV	Not a little comforted	Greatly comforted
Acts 22:3	*At the feet of Gamaliel*	HCSB	At the feet of Gamaliel	ESV	At the feet of Gamaliel	Under Gamaliel
Acts 22:5	*Having been bound*	ESV	In bonds	NKJV	In chains	As prisoners
Rom 6:21[o]	*What fruit?*	HCSB	What fruit?	ESV	What fruit?	What benefit?
Rom 13:13[p]	*Let us walk properly*	ESV	Let us walk properly	NKJV	Let us walk properly	Let us behave properly
1 Cor 4:6[q]	*Be puffed up*	NIV	Be puffed up	ESV	Be puffed up	Become arrogant
2 Cor 6:14	*Unequally yoked*	ESV	Unequally yoked	NKJV	Unequally yoked	Bound together[r]
Col 3:22	*Eyeservice*	ESV	Eye-service	NKJV	Eyeservice	External service
1 Thess 4:2	*Through the Lord Jesus*	HCSB	Through the Lord Jesus	ESV	Through the Lord Jesus	By the authority of the Lord Jesus
2 Tim 2:5	*Is not crowned*	HCSB	Is not crowned	ESV	Is not crowned	Does not win the prize
1 Pet 3:7	*As with a weaker vessel, the female*	ESV	To the woman as the weaker vessel	NKJV	To the wife, as to the weaker vessel	As with someone weaker, since she is a woman

[o] Also Rom 6:22; Phil 4:17.

[p] In 1 Cor 3:3, the situation is reversed. This time the NASB translated the Greek word *peripateō* (περιπατέω) literally as "walking," and the ESV and NKJV interpreted it as "behaving." Compare also 2 Cor 12:18; Col 4:5; 1 Thess 4:12. The NASB footnote for these verses and for Rom 13:13 says, "Lit *walk*," indicating that "walk" is the most literal English representation of *peripateō*.

[q] Also 1 Cor 8:1. The ESV translated it the same as the NASB in 1 Cor 4:18 and 1 Cor 5:2.

[r] The phrase "unequally yoked" in 2 Cor 6:14 represents a single, compound word in Greek, *hetero-zugeō* (ἑτεροζυγέω). The NASB rendering "bound together" does not seem to explicitly include the component of meaning intended by the first part of this word (*hetero*), which indicates a mismatch with something of a different kind or class (cf. Deut 22:10). Evidently, the NASB left that part of the meaning to be deduced from the broader context. So did the NIV, NLT, CEV, NET, TEV and others.

If some of the examples in this chart surprise you, keep reading—because this is only the beginning. We will look at many similar examples as we unfold and examine a number of fundamental issues faced by every Bible translator.

Of course, the NASB is not the only version that frequently translates thought for thought rather than word for word. I started with the NASB since it has been called the "Most Literal." All versions translate thought for thought rather than word for word in many contexts. Some just do it more consistently than others.

We could generate similar lists of thought-for-thought renderings for every literal version. Below is a small sampling of verses where the English Standard Version (ESV)[7] translated thought for thought even though some other versions did not (table 1.4).

Table 1.4

Original Wording[a]		Essentially Literal Rendering				Thought for Thought
		Various Versions				ESV
1 Sam 22:19	*he struck with the edge of the sword*[b]	NASB	he struck . . . with the edge of the sword	NKJV	he struck with the edge of the sword	he put to the sword
Mt 16:23	*You are a **stumbling block** to me*	NIV	You are a **stumbling block** to me	NASB	You are a **stumbling block** to me	You are a **hindrance** to me
Mt 18:6	*causes to **stumble***	NIV	causes . . . to **stumble**	NASB	causes . . . to **stumble**	causes . . . to **sin**[c]
Mk 9:3	*no **cloth refiner** on earth*	HCSB	no **launderer** on earth	NASB	no **launderer** on earth	no **one** on earth
Mk 12:19	***his brother***	HCSB	**his brother**	NKJV	**his brother**	**the man**
Lk 1:34	*since I do not **know a man***	NKJV	since I do not **know a man**	KJV	seeing **I know not a man**	since **I am a virgin**
Jn 9:41	*you would have no **sin***	HCSB	you wouldn't have **sin**	VOICE	you would be without **sin**	you would have no **guilt**

[a] The original wording for these examples is based on footnotes in the ESV.
[b] Lit *mouth of the sword*.
[c] Also Mt 15:8-9.

---

[7] In chapter 2, the charts of Hebrew and Greek figures of speech (tables 2.5 and 2.10), along with their associated footnotes, include more than one hundred instances where the ESV translated thought for thought, even though in a number of those cases, other versions such as the NASB, KJV or NIV aimed for a more word-for-word rendering.

	Essentially Literal Rendering					Thought for Thought
Original Wording[a]	Various Versions					ESV
Acts 17:24	*made by* **hands**	HCSB	made by **hands**	NASB	made with **hands**	made by **man**[d]
Rom 3:20	*no flesh will be justified*	NASB	no **flesh** will be justified	NKJV	no **flesh** will be justified	no **human being** will be justified
1 Cor 1:26	*according to the flesh*	NASB	according to the **flesh**	NKJV	according to the **flesh**	according to **worldly standards**
1 Cor 11:30	*and some have fallen asleep*	NIV	and a number . . . have fallen asleep	NASB	and a number **sleep**	and some have **died**[e]
Eph 4:22	*put off . . . the old man*	HCSB	took off . . . **the old man**	NKJV	put off . . . **the old man**	put off **your** old **self**[f]

[d]See Grudem, "Are Only *Some* Words of Scripture Breathed Out by God?" pp. 35-37, under the heading "The Missing Hands."
[e]Ibid., pp. 21-22, on the figurative use of "sleep" to signify "death."
[f]Also Col 3:9.

My work as a translator brought me to the realization that literal Bible versions in English often take turns being the most (or least) literal among their peers. For example, in table 1.5, we see that sometimes the NASB gave a literal rendering of the Hebrew and Greek words for "flesh"[8] but the ESV replaced them with dynamic equivalents; and in other cases, the ESV gave a literal rendering but the NASB did not.[9]

As I continued comparing English Bible versions, I was shocked to find that not only are literal versions not always literal, but sometimes the notably nonliteral versions are more literal than the so-called literal ones. I found a surprising number of places where meaning-based versions such as the New International Version (NIV)[10] and the New Living Translation (NLT) are more literal than versions that describe themselves as word-for-

[8]See Douglas J. Moo, "'Flesh' in Romans: A Challenge for the Translator," in *The Challenge of Bible Translation*, ed. Glen G. Scorgie, Mark L. Strauss and Steven M. Voth (Grand Rapids: Zondervan, 2003), pp. 365-79.
[9]In the ten verses listed in table 1.5, the HCSB translators translated "flesh" literally just once (Rom 3:20). In the other nine, they used thought-for-thought renderings such as "humanity," "mankind," "creature" or "human perspective."
[10]All quotations from the New International Version (NIV) are taken from the 2011 edition unless otherwise noted.

word translations, such as the NASB and ESV. Below are a few such instances (tables 1.6 through 1.10). We will look at more in later chapters.

Table 1.5

Literal[a]		NASB	ESV
Ps 65:2	*flesh*	men	flesh
Is 66:23	*flesh*	mankind	flesh
Jer 12:12	*flesh*	anyone	flesh
Dan 4:12	*flesh*	living creatures	flesh
Joel 2:28	*flesh*	mankind	flesh
Lev 17:14	*flesh*	flesh	creature
Rom 3:20	*flesh*	flesh	human being
1 Cor 1:26	*flesh*	flesh	worldly standards
Eph 6:5	*flesh*	flesh	earthly
Jude 7	*flesh*	flesh	desire

[a] According to footnotes in the NASB and ESV. The NASB footnotes for the first five examples here say, "Lit *flesh*."

Table 1.6

		Essentially Literal Rendering	Thought for Thought	
Original Wording[a]		NIV	ESV	NASB
Gen 16:6	*your maid is in your **hand**[b]*	your slave is in your **hands**	your servant is in your **power**	your maid is in your **power**
Job 17:13	*I spread out my bed*	I spread out my bed	I make my bed	I make my bed
Prov 24:32	*I set my **heart**[c]*	I applied my **heart**	I considered	I reflected
Is 32:6	*to make **empty** the hungry soul[d]*	the hungry he leaves **empty**	to leave the craving of the hungry **unsatisfied**	to keep the hungry person **unsatisfied**
Lam 2:3	*every **horn** of Israel*	every **horn** of Israel	all the **might** of Israel	all the **strength** of Israel
2 Cor 11:29	*and I do not **burn**?*	and I do not inwardly **burn**?	and I am not **indignant**?	without my **intense concern**?
Col 2:16	*judge you*	judge you	pass judgment on you	act as your judge

[a] The original wording for tables 1.6 through 1.9 is based on footnotes in the NASB.
[b] See Grudem, "Are Only *Some* Words of Scripture Breathed Out by God?" pp. 35-37, under the heading "The Missing Hands."
[c] Ibid., pp. 44-45, under the heading "The Missing Heart."
[d] Ibid., pp. 37-38, under the heading "The Lost Soul."

Table 1.7

		Essentially Literal Rendering			Thought for Thought	
Original Wording		NIV	NLT	GW	ESV	NASB
Ps 69:14	*those who hate me*	those who hate me	those who hate me	those who hate me	my enemies	my foes
Song 3:6	*Who is this?*	**Who** is this?	**Who** is this?	**Who** is this?	**What** is that?	**What** is this?

Table 1.8

		Essentially Literal Rendering	Thought for Thought		
Original Wording		NIV	ESV	NASB	HCSB
Ps 9:4	*my right and my cause*	my right and my cause	my just cause	my just cause	my just cause
Phil 1:14	*my bonds*	my chains	my imprisonment	my imprisonment	my imprisonment

Table 1.9

		Essentially Literal Rendering			Thought for Thought		
Original Wording		NIV	NLT	GW	ESV	NASB	HCSB
Ps 44:14	*shaking of the head*[a]	shake their heads	shake their heads	shake their heads	laughing-stock	laughing-stock	laughing-stock
Prov 14:7	*lips of knowledge*	knowl-edge on their **lips**	knowl-edge on their **lips**	knowl-edge from his **lips**	**words** of knowl-edge	**words** of knowl-edge	knowl-edge from his **speech**

[a] In this case, the meaning-based CEV also opted for a literal rendering: "shake their heads."

Table 1.10

		Essentially Literal Rendering			Thought for Thought
Original Wording[a]		NIV	NLT	GW	HCSB
1 Sam 13:14	*a man according to his **heart***	a man after his own **heart**	a man after his own **heart**	a man after his own **heart**	a man loyal to Him[b]
Is 14:12	*Day Star, **son** of the dawn*	morning star, **son of** the dawn	shining star, **son of** the morning	morning star, **son of** the dawn	Shining morning star
Rom 11:9	*table*	table	table	table	feasting

[a] The original wording for table 1.10 is based on footnotes in the HCSB.
[b] See Grudem, "Are Only *Some* Words of Scripture Breathed Out by God?," pp. 44-45, under the heading "The Missing Heart."

Some authors who prefer literal Bible versions have compiled similar verse-by-verse comparisons,[11] which contrast literal versions with non-literal ones. But I have found that the verses in the preceding charts (tables 1.1 through 1.10) are conspicuously absent from those comparisons.[12]

In most contexts, the ESV and NASB are indeed more literal than the NIV and NLT. However, a truly objective comparison of these versions should include at least a few of the places where "dynamic equivalence"[13] translations such as the NLT and NIV are more literal than the "essentially literal"[14] ESV or the "strictly literal"[15] NASB.

A SOLEMN RESPONSIBILITY

During the years that we served in PNG, I took my job as a Bible translator very seriously. The sobering weight of the task often drove me to my knees in prayer. I had fully committed myself to translating God's Word faithfully and accurately into the Lamogai language. But when I realized how frequently the literal English versions abandoned their own rules, it made my job a bit more perplexing. I found myself asking, "Are literal versions really literal? Why do literal versions translate thought for thought rather than word for word so often—even in places where they do not have to? And how does that relate to faithfulness and accuracy in translation? How is the average reader of a literal Bible version to know which verses are literal and which ones are not?"

In the chapters to follow, we will delve into these and other crucial questions about literalness in translation. At the same time, we will explore

---

[11]Collins, Grudem, Poythress, Ryken and Winter, *Translating Truth*, pp. 31-48, 88, 101, 103. Leland Ryken, *Understanding English Bible Translation: The Case for an Essentially Literal Approach* (Wheaton, IL: Crossway, 2009), pp. 28, 33, 101-2, 106, 164-66. See also www.esv.org, "Verse by Verse Comparisons," ©2005-2008. This page has been removed from the most current version of the ESV website, but copies are available; and www.lockman.org, "How does the NASB compare to other English versions?" © 1999-2013.

[12]Ryken (*Understanding English Bible Translation*, p. 33) did use one of the verses included in table 1.3: Eccles 11:9. However, he did not mention that the NASB set aside the original word *sights* and replaced it with an interpretive substitute, "desires." This rendering is acceptable, but it is not literal, as acknowledged by the NASB translators in their footnote, "Lit *sights*."

[13]www.esv.org, "How is the ESV Different from Other Translations?" ©2005-2008. This page has been removed from the most current version of the ESV website, but copies are available. This web page describes the NIV and the NLT as "dynamic equivalence" translations.

[14]Ibid. This web page describes the ESV as an "essentially literal" translation.

[15]Ibid. This web page describes the NASB as a "strictly literal" translation.

some basic principles of translation theory. We can form reliable conclusions about Bible translation only if we understand the kinds of changes translators make and why they make them.

Most of the scriptural examples in this book are taken from literal English versions. That is intentional because the book's primary focus is literalness in translation. In order to answer the question, Are literal versions really literal? we need to look at the way those literal versions translated some of the words and phrases of Scripture. Also, as we consider dynamic equivalence translation principles, it will become apparent that it is not necessary to use dynamic equivalence versions to illustrate those principles, because every literal version uses classic dynamic equivalence principles in many contexts.[16]

FROM ENMITY TO AMITY

Living among the Lamogai people of PNG, we saw the unifying power of God's Word accomplish miracles that we sometimes doubted would ever come to fruition. The Lamogai people were such a proud people—fierce, unflinching and often arrogant. They prided themselves on being some of the most brutal warriors throughout that entire district. In the past, there was mutual hatred and fear between the Lamogai people and the other tribal groups that lived around them. But as the gospel began to penetrate Lamogai society, it was breaking into several of the surrounding tribes as well.

In recent years, the Lamogai believers have hosted Christian conferences that were attended by believers from ten or more tribal groups. Many of those with whom they now enjoy Christian fellowship are direct descendants of their parents' and grandparents' archenemies.

Historically, no neighboring tribe was more feared or more hated than the notorious Loko tribe. The Lamogais referred to them as the Amolou people, a word akin to the Lamogai word for "enemy." The relationship between the Lamogai and Loko tribes was one of perpetual warfare. What a difference it is now to see enthusiastic, young Bible teachers from these two

---

[16]See D. A. Carson, *The King James Version Debate: A Plea for Realism* (Grand Rapids: Baker Book House, 1979), p. 90. Carson states, "it ought to be obvious that to some extent *every* translation, from *anywhere* on the spectrum, is necessarily involved again and again with finding the 'dynamic equivalent.'"

tribes build deep, enduring friendships. For these tribal believers, the Word of God is not an instrument of division but of unity only. Living in the seclusion of their jungle refuge, they remain untouched by the distant controversy surrounding standards of translation. While the Word of God was uniting violent, tribal enemies on one side of the world, it was becoming an ever-increasing source of disagreement among their civilized, suburbanite brothers and sisters living in the opposite hemisphere.

2

FORM AND MEANING

INNOCENT BYSTANDERS AT THE
CENTER OF THE DEBATE

♦ ♦ ♦

For verily I say unto you, Till heaven and earth pass,
one jot or one tittle shall in no wise pass
from the law, till all be fulfilled.

MATTHEW 5:18 (KJV)

Unless you speak intelligible words with your tongue,
how will anyone know what you are saying?
You will just be speaking into the air.
Undoubtedly there are all sorts of languages in the world,
yet none of them is without meaning.

1 CORINTHIANS 14:9-10 (NIV)

Much of the translation debate among English-speaking Christians today centers on the connection between form and meaning.[1] The form

---

[1] See Gordon D. Fee and Mark L. Strauss, *How to Choose a Translation for All Its Worth* (Grand Rapids: Zondervan, 2007), pp. 28-30.

includes the letters, words, phrases, sentences, paragraphs, and so on. The meaning consists of the concepts or thoughts associated with each of the forms. Both elements are essential in all communication.

Since form and meaning are both integral, it could be difficult to argue that one is more important than the other. In every language, there is an inseparable partnership between the two. Each form is worthless without its meaning, and meaning can be communicated only by some kind of form.

In the original manuscripts of the Bible, it is the meaning of the message that imparts life. Yet without the form to act as a conduit, there would be no message. But how does this linguistic duo relate to the practice of translation? Should translators try to translate the form or the meaning?

REFLECTING THE ORIGINAL FORM

There are various kinds of Bible versions in the English language. Some place a high priority on trying to reflect the form of the original. Yet every Bible translator knows it is impossible to reflect 100 percent of the original form in English or any other language. Translation by its definition means changing the form.[2] In order for any kind of message to be translated, it must be changed from the form of one language into the form of another language.[3]

So it is not a question of whether or not translators should change the form. If they do not change the form, they have not translated. The question is, How much of the original form should they try to reflect in their translations? In Scripture, even the Hebrew[4] and Greek[5] letters themselves are part of the original form (table 2.1).[6] Obviously, if translators keep the Hebrew and Greek letters, they have not translated.

---

[2]See Mildred L. Larson, *Meaning-Based Translation: A Guide to Cross-Language Equivalence*, rev. ed. (Lanham, MD: University Press of America, 1998), p. 1.

[3]The word *translate* is defined in the *Cambridge Dictionary* as "to change something into a new form" (Cambridge: Cambridge University Press, 2013); and in the Merriam-Webster Online Dictionary a "change from one . . . form or appearance to another."

[4]The word *Hebrew* as it is used here and throughout this book refers specifically to the ancient Hebrew language of the Old Testament.

[5]The word *Greek* as it is used here and throughout this book refers specifically to first-century *koine* Greek, the language of the New Testament.

[6]Jill Goring, NTM Team Translation Workshop.

Table 2.1

Genesis 1:1	Matthew 1:1
בְּרֵאשִׁית בָּרָא אֱלֹהִים אֵת הַשָּׁמַיִם וְאֵת הָאָרֶץ	Βίβλος γενέσεως Ἰησοῦ Χριστοῦ υἱοῦ Δαυὶδ υἱοῦ Ἀβραάμ.

In order for genuine translation to take place, two things must happen: The meaning must remain the same, and the form must change (at least to some degree). If either of these two things does not happen, we have not translated. In saying that the form must change, I am not implying that no part of the original form can or should be reflected in the translation. Some sense of the form of the original will be apparent in every translation of Scripture.

THE PROCESS OF TRANSLATION

Some translation theorists have used a meaning-based model[7] like the one in figure 2.1 to illustrate the translation process. According to the theory described in this model, the translator would start with the form of the source language text and dig beneath the surface to discover the meaning. The translator then searches for the best way to re-express this same meaning using appropriate forms in the target or receptor

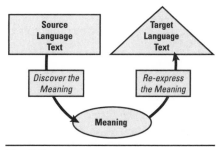

Fig. 2.1.

language. This second step of re-expressing the meaning is where translation takes place. This model is based on the premise that meaning has priority over form.[8]

Historically, this model has been mainly associated with dynamic equiv-

---

[7]Larson, *Meaning-Based Translation*, p. 4, display 1.1; see also Katharine Barnwell, *Introduction to Semantics and Translation* (Horsleys Green, UK: Summer Institute of Linguistics, 1974, 1980), p. 14.

[8]Eugene A. Nida and Charles R. Taber, *The Theory and Practice of Translation* (Leiden: E. J. Brill, 1982), p. 13.

alence or meaning-based translations rather than literal translations. Yet I believe if we carefully examine the issues involved in translation, we will see that this model illustrates the underlying approach used by the translators of *every* English version—including the more literal ones. The evidence suggests that all translators use this same basic process. The difference lies in the way they apply the process.

In response to the rise in popularity of dynamic equivalence translation, the antithetical term "formal equivalence"[9] was coined. It seems reasonable that the formal equivalence[10] translation method could be illustrated by a modified version of the dynamic equivalence model. Formal

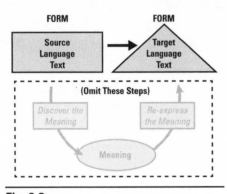

Fig. 2.2.

equivalence would presumably omit the discovery and re-expression of meaning and simply transfer the form of the source language to the form of the target language (figure 2.2).

Is this really the model that the translators of literal versions followed? As we look at the evidence, I believe it will become clear that it would be impossible for any translator to consistently follow this form-to-form model and still produce an understandable translation. While meaning is universal[11]—reproducible in all languages—form is different in every language. Therefore, consistent formal equivalence, in the truest sense of the term, does not exist between any two languages on earth.

[9]In using the term "formal equivalence" here, I refer to the original words themselves—not the word order of the original. See Wayne Grudem, "Are Only *Some* Words of Scripture Breathed Out by God? Why Plenary Inspiration Favors 'Essentially Literal' Bible Translation," in C. John Collins, Wayne Grudem, Vern Sheridan Poythress, Leland Ryken and Bruce Winter, *Translating Truth: The Case for Essentially Literal Bible Translation* (Wheaton, IL: Crossway, 2005), p. 20.

[10]Also called verbal-equivalence translation. See Leland Ryken, *Understanding English Bible Translation: The Case for an Essentially Literal Approach* (Wheaton, IL: Crossway, 2009), p. 73.

[11]Cf. Larson, *Meaning-Based Translation*, p. 1.

THE IDIOM DISCONNECT

In order to better understand this point, let us consider the relationship between meaning and form in idioms.[12] As you learned in your high school English class, an idiom is an expression which means something different than the usual sense of its individual words. Anyone fluent in more than one living language has probably encountered humorous situations where a speaker tried to translate an idiom literally.

During the years that my wife and I worked with the Lamogai people, we served alongside several missionary coworkers. One couple we served with was Jan and Annette from the Netherlands, whose native tongue is Dutch. On more than one occasion when I was carrying on a conversation with Jan, out of the blue, he would say something in English that sounded to me like nonsense. When that happened, I would have to ask him to repeat it. Even though he was using English words that were familiar to me, I did not have a clue what he was trying to say. Then it would dawn on me that he was translating a Dutch idiom literally into English. (I wish I had written some of them down!) When I would point that out to him, he would say, "Oh, don't you say it that way in English?"

The disconnect between English and Dutch idioms went both ways. Though Jan and Annette speak English very well, they sometimes stumbled over our North American idioms. I remember one time several of us were having a casual conversation, and someone said, "They spilled the beans." Jan quietly turned to me and said, "Spilled the beans? What does that mean?" "Oh," I said, "that means they let the cat out of the bag."

Idioms lend richness and variety to every language—including the biblical languages. The problems associated with appropriately translating idioms provide a unique challenge for translators.

DIRECT TRANSFER IS RARE

It is rare that an idiom can be translated directly from one language to another, unless the two languages are closely related or have a common origin. Of all the picturable idioms that I am familiar with in English and Lamogai, I can think of only two that translate clearly between the two languages.

---

[12]Cf. Fee and Strauss, *How to Choose a Translation*, pp. 61-75.

In English, we sometimes say, "My head is splitting." It just so happens that a literal translation of this idiom into Lamogai (*apungu navak*) carries exactly the same meaning that it does in English: I have a terrible headache.

Another idiom that translates straight across between Lamogai and English is the phrase "it turns my stomach." A literal translation of this idiom into Lamogai (*vavluk peleinong*) has the same meaning as its English counterpart: It nauseates me.

When we were learning the Lamogai language, we were surprised to stumble on these two idioms that can be translated literally between English and Lamogai. It is much more common to find that idioms and figures of speech do not line up between two such unrelated languages.

For example, in English we use the metaphor "mouth of the river" to refer to a river's outlet—the place where it pours out into another body of water. The Lamogai language also uses the phrase "mouth of the river" (*uri auna*). But in Lamogai, "mouth of the river" means the bank of the river, running all the way down both sides, not the outlet as in English.

"Autumn Days": An Example from Hebrew

What picture comes to your mind when you hear the phrase "in my autumn days"? For most English speakers it evokes an image of an elderly person heading into the final season of life. But that is not what this Hebrew phrase means in Job 29:4. The New American Standard Bible (NASB) translated it "in the prime of my days." The New International Version (NIV) and English Standard Version (ESV) both translated it "in my prime." The word *autumn* in this Hebrew metaphor[13] refers to the time of greatest fruitfulness. It represents the stage in a person's life when he or she is producing a bountiful harvest. The King James Version (KJV) translated it "in the days of my youth."[14] This seems strangely ironic, because it is the opposite of the image called to mind by the English phrase "my autumn days."

The translators of every major English version recognized the fact that a literal, word-for-word translation of the form of this metaphor would

---

[13]The NASB footnote for Job 29:4 says, "Lit *the days of my autumn*"; the ESV footnote says, "Hebrew *my autumn days*." Both of these versions translated this Hebrew word as "autumn" in Prov 20:4. They translated it "winter" in all other contexts (Gen 8:22; Ps 74:17; Jer 36:22; Amos 3:15; Zech 14:8).

[14]Also the Holman Christian Standard Bible (HCSB).

distort the meaning of God's Word. Therefore, in this context, they wisely chose to abandon the form of the original words in order to communicate the meaning of the phrase. This is very similar to the practice of paraphrasing, which is "giving the meaning in another form."[15]

In translation, it is often necessary to set aside form in order to preserve meaning. But as we will see through many examples, it is never appropriate to set aside meaning in order to reflect the original form. This is the rationale behind the basic translation premise: Meaning has priority over form. Again, that is not to say that form is unimportant. But in situations where a choice must be made between reflecting the form or preserving the meaning, meaning consistently takes priority—even in the most literal versions of the Bible.

In contrast, formal equivalence translation, taken to its logical end, would presumably be built on the premise that form has priority over meaning. However, I have never seen a Bible version in English or any other language that was consistently built on this kind of translation principle.

THE EDGE OF THE SWORD

Let us consider another Hebrew example. In English, when we refer to the sharpened blade of a sword, we usually say the "edge of the sword." That is how most English versions translate it. The Hebrew language of the Old Testament, however, uses a metaphor to express this meaning: the "mouth of the sword."[16] I do not know of any English version that translated this Hebrew metaphor literally. But the Lamogai language uses this same metaphor. In Lamogai, as in Hebrew, the sharpened blade of a sword is called the mouth of the sword (*lungai auna*). Since the form of this Lamogai metaphor literally reflects the form of the Hebrew words (table 2.2), does that mean the Lamogai translation of this phrase is more faithful than that of our English versions? No, I do not believe it does. Lamogai and English have equally conveyed completely the original meaning. It happens, in this case, that Lamogai gives a closer, word-for-word translation of the Hebrew form than English does.

---

[15]"Paraphrase," Merriam-Webster Online Dictionary, www.merriam-webster.com.
[16]Gen 34:26; Ex 17:13; Num 21:24; Deut 13:15 (twice); 20:13; Josh 6:21; 8:24 (twice); 10:28, 30, 32, 35, 37, 39; 11:11, 12, 14; 19:47; Judg 1:8, 25; 4:15, 16; 18:27; 20:37, 48; 21:10; 1 Sam 15:8; 22:19 (twice); 2 Sam 15:14; 2 Kings 10:25; Job 1:15, 17; Jer 21:7.

Table 2.2

English	Hebrew	Lamogai
edge of the sword	mouth of the sword לְפִי־חָרֶב	mouth of the sword *(lungai auna)*

So we see that increased literalness does not necessarily result in increased accuracy. If it did, we would need to change "edge of the sword" to "mouth of the sword" in all our English versions. However, that kind of literalness would likely decrease the accuracy of the translation, not increase it.

WARM HEARTS: AN EXAMPLE FROM LAMOGAI

In English we describe a compassionate and kind person as warmhearted. The word *warmhearted* can be translated literally into Lamogai (*antoine ingil*). But the problem is that in Lamogai, "warmhearted" means "angry," as though the person were boiling inside. Obviously, that would not be a faithful or accurate translation of the English word *warmhearted*. If we use the form-to-form translation model to illustrate this example, it would look like figure 2.3.

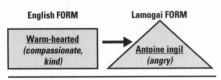

Fig. 2.3.

A related English figure is "coldhearted," which means "ruthless" and "cruel." Again, it is possible to translate this figure literally into Lamogai (*antoine vris*), but as you might expect, "coldhearted" in Lamogai is the opposite of "warmhearted." It means the person is no longer angry. He is appeased, placated, pacified. He has cooled down from his boiling anger (figure 2.4).

A third related English figure[17] is "hardhearted," which means "stubborn" and "unteachable," as

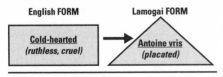

Fig. 2.4.

---

[17]Another related figure in this series is "tenderhearted." Interestingly, Hebrew uses this same figure but with a completely different meaning than in English. In 2 Chron 13:7, the NASB translated the word *tenderhearted* as "timid," the ESV translated it "irresolute," the NIV translated it "indecisive" and the HCSB translated it "inexperienced." Also, the figure "heavy-hearted" has a different meaning in Hebrew than in English. In Ex 7:14, where the Hebrew text says "Pharaoh is *heavy* of heart," the NASB translated it "Pharaoh's heart is *stubborn*."

in Proverbs 28:14 (NASB), which says, "he who hardens his heart[18] will fall into calamity." This illustrates a different kind of translation problem. Historically, a literal translation of "hardhearted" into Lamogai (*antoine namor*) would be meaningless. Rather than trying to match the form of the words, the translator needs to dig beneath the surface and identify the real meaning of the phrase. In English, when we say "his heart is hardened," we are saying "he is stubborn and unteachable." Now that the translator has determined the actual meaning of the phrase, the next step is to determine how that same meaning can be naturally communicated in the target language.

In Lamogai, instead of saying "his heart is hardened," they would say "his ears are closed" (*veine kauk*). The meaning of this Lamogai phrase is virtually identical to the meaning of the English phrase "his heart is hardened." If we apply this example to the translation model we looked at earlier, it would look something like the illustration in figure 2.5.

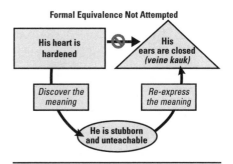

Fig. 2.5.

In this example, we have substituted a completely different body part—ears in place of heart. Is that acceptable, or would that be a distortion of God's Word? In order to shed more light on this question, let's look at a parallel example where one body part is substituted for another.

SUBSTITUTING A DIFFERENT BODY PART

When we talk about the seat of human emotions in English, we often speak of the heart. Many other languages use a different body part to express this concept. In Job 19:27, the NASB reads, "My heart faints within me." In some languages, when translators translated the seat of the emotions and intellect, they substituted a different, culturally appropriate body part. Consider the example in table 2.3.

---

[18]See also Ex 4:21; 7:3, 13, 22; 8:15, 19, 32; 9:7, 12, 34, 35; 10:1, 20, 27; 11:10; 14:4, 8, 17; Deut 15:7; Josh 11:20; 1 Sam 6:6; 2 Chron 36:13; Job 41:24; Ps 95:8; Is 63:17; Mk 6:52; 8:17; Jn 12:40; Heb 3:8, 15; 4:7.

Table 2.3

	NASB	Another Language
Job 19:27	My *heart* faints within me!	My *kidneys* faint within me!
Ps 16:7	my *mind* instructs me.	my *kidneys* instruct me.
Ps 73:21	I was pierced *within*	I was pierced in my *kidneys*
Ps 139:13	You formed my *inward parts*	You formed my *kidneys*

Is this type of change appropriate? Can the seat of emotions and intellect be represented by the word *kidneys* in one language and *heart* in another? You may be surprised to know that the language using the word *kidneys* in this example is Hebrew. The NASB rendering in English is the cultural adaptation. It is not the other way around.

All four verses in table 2.3 use the common Hebrew word for "kidneys" (*kilyah*).[19] This Old Testament word occurs several times in its nonfigurative sense in the context of offering animal sacrifices. For example, Leviticus 9:10 (ESV) says, "the fat and the kidneys (*kilyah*) . . . he burned on the altar." In cases like this, every English version translated it "kidneys." When this word occurs in its figurative sense, however, the translators of most versions chose not to translate it literally. Instead, they used meaningful, culturally appropriate substitutes. They translated the thought(s) or concept(s) rather than the primary sense of the word.

The NASB translated the figurative sense of this Hebrew word six different ways in various contexts (table 2.4). The ESV translated it four ways, interpreting Lamentations 3:13 to be nonfigurative. In the New Testament, the word *kidneys* occurs only once. It is the Greek word *nephros*[20] in Revelation 2:23.

The ESV and NASB translations are described in their own introductions[21] as literal versions, translated word for word. Yet they allowed themselves quite a bit of leeway in translating this Hebrew concept several different ways: "heart," "mind," "inward parts," "inmost being."[22] Also, these two

---

[19] *The Brown-Driver-Briggs Hebrew and English Lexicon* (Peabody, MA: Hendrickson, 1996) defines this word as "kidneys: a) of physical organ (lit.); b) of seat of emotion and affection (fig.); c) of sacrificial animals."

[20] This is the word from which we get our English word *nephritis* ("inflammation of the kidney").

[21] See the introduction to the ESV (www.esv.org) and the introduction to the NASB (www.lockman.org).

[22] The HCSB also translated it "emotions" and "conscience" in some contexts.

Table 2.4

	NASB	ESV	Hebrew
Job 19:27	heart	heart	*kidneys*
Ps 7:9	minds	hearts	*kidneys*
Ps 16:7	mind	heart	*kidneys*
Ps 26:2	mind	heart	*kidneys*
Ps 73:21	within	heart	*kidneys*
Ps 139:13	inward parts	inward parts	*kidneys*
Prov 23:16	inmost being	inmost being	*kidneys*
Jer 11:20	feelings	heart	*kidneys*
Jer 12:2	mind	heart	*kidneys*
Jer 17:10	mind	mind	*kidneys*
Jer 20:12	mind	heart	*kidneys*
Lam 3:13	inward parts	kidneys	*kidneys*
	NASB	ESV	Greek
Rev 2:23	minds	mind	*kidneys*

fairly literal versions are quite different from each other in their translation of this word.[23] Sometimes they both translated it "heart." Sometimes they both translated it "mind." Sometimes the ESV translated it "heart," while the NASB translated it "mind," "within" or "feelings." In every case, the primary sense of the word in the original is "kidneys." Therefore, the various NASB and ESV renderings of these verses are purely a matter of interpretation on the part of translators. All of these interpretive renderings are acceptable, but none are based on the principle of formal equivalence.

A More Literal Alternative

The translators of the King James Version took a different approach. They translated the figurative sense of this Hebrew word as "reins," which is an archaic English word for "kidneys." It comes from the Latin word *renes*[24]

---

[23]The NASB's default translation of "kidneys" (Heb *kilyāh*; Gk *nephros*) is "mind," translating it "heart" only once; the ESV's default translation is "heart," translating it "mind" only where "kidneys" (*kilyāh*, *nephros*) and "heart" (Heb *lēb*; Gk *kardia*) occur together as a conjoined pair. It would not make sense to say "the heart and the heart," so the ESV translated it "the mind and the heart." In some contexts, the word order seems to indicate that the ESV translated the word for "kidneys" (*kilyāh*, *nephros*) as "heart" and the word for "heart" (*lēb*, *kardia*) as "mind." See Ps 7:9; 26:2; Jer 11:20; 17:10; 20:12; Rev 2:23.

[24]The French word *rein* and the Italian word *rene* still closely reflect the Latin form.

("kidneys"), from which we get the present-day medical term *renal*, defined as "relating to . . . the kidneys."[25] For example, renal function equals kidney function, renal failure equals kidney failure, and renal transplant equals kidney transplant.

The KJV's strategy for translating this Hebrew word was quite innovative, but it created a problem that the translators did not foresee. In English, the little-known term *reins* ("kidneys") has sometimes been confused with the unrelated homophone *reins,* which is "a strap . . . by which a rider or driver controls an animal (from Latin *retinere* to restrain)."[26] The phonetic correspondence between *reins* (kidneys) and *reins* (for controlling animals) is purely coincidental. The words have completely separate origins.

True as this is, it did not keep one preacher from drawing a connection between these two words when expounding on the significance of the word *reins* in the KJV. A well-intentioned Bible teacher from Scotland (God rest his soul) gave this explanation:

> What, you may well ask, constitutes a man's *reins*? *Reins*, as you all know are used to direct animals (horses, donkeys, bullocks, camels and sledge dogs). Without *reins* a rider has virtually no power over the horse he is riding or the team he is driving. *Reins* are lines of communication between man and animal, between God and man. *Reins* give total control.[27]

If this preacher had understood the real meaning of the word *reins* the way the KJV translators understood it, this sermon would have taken on a completely new significance. It might have read like this:

> What, you may well ask, constitutes a man's *kidneys*? *Kidneys*, as you all know are used to direct animals (horses, donkeys, bullocks, camels and sledge dogs). Without *kidneys* a rider has virtually no power over the horse he is riding or the team he is driving. *Kidneys* are lines of communication between man and animal, between God and man. *Kidneys* give total control.

The KJV rendering *reins* is not wrong. This word carries exactly the same meaning as the Hebrew and Greek words it represents. The problem is that

---

[25]Merriam-Webster Online Dictionary.
[26]Ibid.
[27]David B. Loughran, Stewarton Bible School, Stewarton, Scotland, 1998 (italics added).

most English readers are not familiar with this meaning of the word *reins*. The meaning-based (or dynamic equivalence) terms used by the NASB and ESV ("heart," "mind," "inmost being," "feelings") do a better job of communicating the true sense of the Hebrew word *kilyāh* ("kidneys").

These examples support the idea that increased literalness does not necessarily equate to increased faithfulness and accuracy. In addition, they demonstrate the fact that every English version, including the more literal ones, must at times abandon the primary sense of the original words and translate the underlying thought(s) or concept(s) instead.

This raises an important question: Why, in the case of idioms and figures of speech, is it often acceptable for the translators of all versions to abandon the literal form of the words? The answer is clear: because keeping the form would distort the meaning. That is the logic behind the axiom, Meaning has priority over form.

THE DYNAMICS OF MEANING

When we talk about the dynamics[28] of meaning in translation, we refer to the subtle nuances or connotations of the message. When translators aim to match the dynamics of the original, they are attempting to make their translation carry the same emphasis, the same force and intensity, the same tone, the same level of sensitivity and the same degree of appropriateness that the original does. A parallel use of the term *dynamics* is in music, where it refers to the varying levels of softness and loudness within a musical piece. Lack of attention to the dynamics can make a piece of music sound dull and mechanical.

The translators of every English version have frequently given priority to the dynamics of meaning because they know that these subtle nuances are part of the orginal message of Scripture. If the original text is forceful, the translation should be forceful; if the original text is gentle, the translation should be gentle; if the original is humorous, the translation should be humorous; if the original is serious, the translation should be serious. If translators do not get the dynamics right, they may cause the translation to be weak or deficient. Or they may make the

---

[28]See John Beekman and John Callow, *Translating the Word of God* (Grand Rapids: Zondervan, 1974), pp. 39-44.

translation sound stronger than the author intended. They may change the tone of the passage. If the dynamics are not translated correctly, the inspired meaning will be changed.

A Truly Dynamic Phrase

There are many places in Scripture where translators have set aside the goal of reflecting the original words in order to match the dynamics of the meaning. One such case is the KJV phrase, "God forbid!" This is an excellent translational choice for the contexts in which it is used, but it is not literal. The Greek sentence used in these contexts does not include the word for "God" or the word for "forbid." But as we have already seen in other examples, increased literalness does not necessarily equate to increased faithfulness or accuracy. Instead, the KJV rendering "God forbid" seems very much like a paraphrase—interpreting the overarching meaning of the phrase rather than translating the individual words within the phrase. One of the places this KJV expression is found is in Romans 6:1-2: "What shall we say then? Shall we continue in sin, that grace may abound? God forbid."

The phrase "God forbid" occurs fifteen times in the King James New Testament.[29] In every case it is used to translate the Greek phrase *mē genoito*, which could be translated "may it not become," "let it not come to pass," or a number of other similar renderings. The KJV translators chose to replace this Greek phrase with a common British expression of their day.[30]

Why would the KJV replace "may it not be" with the phrase "God forbid"? I believe it is all about the dynamics of the meaning. I am convinced that the King James translators were familiar enough with Greek to know that a literal translation of *mē genoito* could potentially be weak and deficient. It could lose some of the punch that the original author intended, sounding something like this: "What shall we say then? Shall we continue in sin, that grace may abound? Nah, let's not do that, okay?"

The King James translators were fully aware that the meaning of the original includes more than just the words themselves; it also includes the intensity behind those words. They understood the dynamics of the

---

[29]Lk 20:16; Rom 3:4, 6, 31; 6:2, 15; 7:7, 13; 9:14; 11:1, 11; 1 Cor 6:15; Gal 2:17; 3:21; 6:14.
[30]See Ryken, *Understanding English Bible Translation*, pp. 74-75, under the heading "Allegiance to Audience versus Allegiance to Author."

meaning. The phrase "God forbid" is a classic example of dynamic equivalence translation in the KJV.

Most other versions also chose to go with a dynamic interpretation of this Greek sentence, but they used contemporary English phrases rather than the somewhat outdated phrase "God forbid."

KJV: *God forbid.*	ESV: *By no means!*
NKJV: *Certainly not!*	HCSB: *Absolutely not!*
NLT: *Of course not!*	CEV: *No, we should not!*
NCV: *No!*	GW: *That's unthinkable!*

None of these versions tried to achieve formal equivalence when they translated this Greek phrase. They translated thought for thought rather than word for word in order to reflect the dynamics of the original. In this case, the translators of the NASB chose to translate the original words quite literally—using the phrase "May it never be!"—although they too made some adjustments purely for the sake of the dynamics of the meaning. In order to increase the forcefulness of this phrase, they replaced "not" with "never" and inserted an exclamation mark.[31]

The translation of this Greek phrase (*mē genoito*) into English suggests another important principle of translation: The dynamics of the meaning are an essential part of the original message of Scripture. And at least in this case, the translators of most English versions concluded that the dynamics of the meaning take priority over a literal translation of the original words.

FIGURATIVE LANGUAGE IN HEBREW

There are countless idioms and figures of speech in Scripture. Consider the following examples from Hebrew (table 2.5) and the way these four versions translated them. I used gray shading in this chart to mark renderings that depart significantly from the form of the original. A white background indicates that some significant part of the rendering is literal.[32]

---

[31]The YLT also translated this phrase quite literally as "let it not be!"

[32]This chart is only a small sampling of Hebrew figures of speech used in Scripture. See also Wayne Leman, "Hebrew Bible Idioms and Other Figures of Speech," http://bible-translation.110mb.com/otidioms.htm; also http://betterbibles.com.

Table 2.5

Hebrew Figures of Speech[a]		NASB	KJV	ESV	NIV
Gen 20:16	*Covering of eyes*	Your vindication	A covering of the eyes	A sign of your innocence	To cover the offense against you
Gen 30:3	*Give birth on my knees*	Bear on my knees	Bear upon my knees	Give birth on my behalf	Bear children for me
Gen 30:3	*Be built up*	Have children	Have children	Have children	Build a family
Gen 31:20	*Stole the heart of* [b]	Deceived	Stole away unawares	Tricked	Deceived
Gen 38:21	*Sacred woman*	Temple prostitute	Harlot	Cult prostitute	Shrine prostitute
Gen 41:40	*Kiss the ground* [c]	Do homage	Be ruled	Order themselves	Submit
Gen 50:23	*Born on [his] knees*	Born on [his] knees	Brought up upon [his] knees	Counted as [his] own	Placed at birth on [his] knees
Ex 12:6	*Between the two evenings*	At twilight	In the evening	At twilight	At twilight
Ex 34:28[d]	*The ten words*	The Ten Commandments	The Ten Commandments	The Ten Commandments	The Ten Commandments
Lev 19:23	*Uncircumcision*	Forbidden	Uncircumcised	Forbidden	Forbidden
Num 12:11	*Lay sin upon us*	Account . . . sin to us	Lay . . . sin upon us	Punish us	Hold against us . . . sin
Deut 11:10	*Watered it with your feet*	Water it with your foot	Wateredst it with thy foot	Irrigated it	Irrigated it by foot
Deut 22:30	*Skirt*	Skirt	Skirt	Nakedness	Bed
Deut 32:14	*Kidney fat of wheat*	Finest of the wheat	Fat of kidneys of wheat	Very finest of the wheat	Finest kernels of wheat
Judg 8:3	*Their spirit* [e]	Their anger	Their anger	Their anger	Their resentment
Judg 17:5	*Filled the hand* [f]	Consecrated	Consecrated	Ordained	Installed
1 Sam 2:29	*Kick at*	Kick at	Kick . . . at	Scorn	Scorn

[a] Most of the Hebrew translations in this chart were taken from the ESV footnotes for these verses.

[b] See Grudem, "Are Only *Some* Words of Scripture Breathed Out by God?" pp. 44-45, under the heading "The Missing Heart."

[c] Ibid., pp. 43-44, under the heading "The Lost Kiss."

[d] Also many other places throughout the Old Testament.

[e] See Grudem, "Are Only *Some* Words of Scripture Breathed Out by God?" pp. 38-39, under the heading "The Lost Spirit."

[f] Ibid., pp. 35-37, under the heading "The Missing Hands."

Hebrew Figures of Speech[a]		NASB	KJV	ESV	NIV
1 Sam 14:14	*Yoke*	Acre	Acre ... which a yoke of oxen might plow	Acre	Acre
1 Sam 24:3	*Cover his feet*[g]	Relieve himself	Cover his feet	Relieve himself	Relieve himself
2 Sam 20:6	*Snatch away our eyes*	Escape from our sight	Escape us	Escape from us	Escape from us
2 Kings 25:27	*Lifted up the head*	Released	Did lift up the head	Graciously freed	Released
2 Chron 13:7	*Soft of heart*[h]	Timid	Tenderhearted	Irresolute	Indecisive
Job 41:28	*Son of the bow*	Arrow	Arrow	Arrow	Arrows
Ps 30:9	*Blood*	Blood	Blood	Death	Silenced
Ps 94:21		Death			Death
Ps 41:3	*Turn all his bed in his illness*	In his illness ... restore him to health	Make all his bed in his sickness	In his illness ... restore him to health	Restores them from their bed of illness
Ps 44:14	*Shaking of the head*	Laughingstock	Shaking of the head	Laughingstock	Shake their heads
Ps 73:26	*Rock*	Strength	Strength	Strength	Strength
Ps 78:42	*Hand*[i]	Power	Hand	Power	Power
Ps 136:15	*Shook off*	Overthrew	Overthrew	Overthrew	Swept
Ps 141:8	*Pour out my soul*[j]	Leave me defenseless	Leave ... my soul destitute	Leave me ... defenseless	Give me over to death
Prov 2:16	*Foreign woman*	Adulteress	Stranger	Adulteress	Wayward woman
Prov 3:8	*Navel*	Body	Navel	Flesh	Body
Prov 3:25	*Storm*	Onslaught	Desolation	Ruin	Ruin
Prov 5:3	*Palate*	Speech	Mouth	Speech	Speech
Prov 5:19	*Led astray*	Exhilarated	Ravished	Intoxicated	Intoxicated

[g] Cf. Mark L. Strauss, *Distorting Scripture? The Challenge of Bible Translation and Gender Accuracy* (Downers Grove, IL: InterVarsity Press, 1998), p. 82.

[h] See Grudem, "Are Only *Some* Words of Scripture Breathed Out by God?" pp. 44-45, under the heading "The Missing Heart."

[i] Ibid., pp. 35-37, under the heading "The Missing Hands."

[j] Ibid., pp. 37-38, under the heading "The Lost Soul."

Hebrew Figures of Speech[a]		NASB	KJV	ESV	NIV
Prov 12:17	*Breathes out*	Speaks	Speaketh	Speaks	Witness
Prov 15:30	*Makes fat*	Puts fat on	Maketh . . . fat	Refreshes	Gives health to
Prov 16:27	*What is on his lips*	His words	In his lips	His speech	On their lips
Prov 18:5	*Lift the face*[k]	Show partiality	Accept the person	Be partial	Be partial
Prov 23.6	*Eye is evil*	Selfish	Evil eye	Stingy	Begrudging
Prov 28:17	*The pit*	Death	The pit	Death	Grave
Prov 31:8	*Sons of passing away*	Unfortunate	Appointed to destruction	Destitute	Destitute
Eccles 1:2	*Vapor*	Vanity	Vanity	Vanity	Meaningless
Song 2:4	*House of wine*	Banquet hall	Banqueting house	Banqueting house	Banquet hall
Is 6:10	*Fat*	Insensitive	Fat	Dull	Calloused
Is 13:18	*Dash in pieces*	Mow down	Dash . . . to pieces	Slaughter	Strike down
Is 23:5	*Labor pains*	Anguish	Sorely pained	Anguish	Anguish
Is 40:2	*Speak to the heart*[l]	Speak kindly	Speak ye comfortably	Speak tenderly	Speak tenderly
Is 60:5	*Heart . . . tremble and be wide*	Heart . . . thrill and rejoice	Heart . . . fear, and be enlarged	Heart . . . thrill and exalt	Heart . . . throb and swell with joy
Is 65:22	*Wear out*	Wear out	Long enjoy	Long enjoy	Long enjoy
Jer 2:16	*Grazed (fed on grass)*	Shaved	Broken	Shaved	Cracked
Jer 17:5	*Arm*	Strength	Arm	Strength	Strength
Jer 31:20	*Bowels*	Heart	Bowels	Heart	Heart
Ezek 16:25	*Spreading your legs*	Spread your legs	Opened thy feet	Offering yourself	Spreading your legs
Ezek 20:5	*I lifted my hand*[m]	I swore	I . . . lifted up mine hand	I swore	I swore with uplifted hand
Ex 6:8			I did swear		
Obad 1:12	*Enlarge your mouth*	Boast	Spoken proudly	Boast	Boast

[k] Ibid., pp. 41-42, under the heading "The Lost Faces."

[l] Ibid., pp. 44-45, under the heading "The Missing Heart."

[m] Ibid., pp. 35-37, under the heading "The Missing Hands." In order to make that argument more complete and more objective, perhaps it would be good to include this example where the NIV (also VOICE and GW) literally reflected the word *hand* but the ESV and NASB did not.

The New International Version (NIV) is usually the least literal of these four versions, but interestingly, the NIV translated some of these figures of speech more literally than the other versions did. For example, in Psalm 44:14, the NIV literally translated the phrase "shaking the head" from Hebrew,[33] but the NASB and ESV both changed it to "laughingstock."[34] I am not questioning the way the NASB and ESV translated this phrase. I am only pointing out that sometimes literal versions like the NASB and ESV chose to use a meaning-based, thought-for-thought rendering even though a more literal, word-for-word translation was possible, as demonstrated by the NIV rendering.[35]

There is another feature of the NIV renderings that I find interesting. In some cases, the NIV translators found creative ways to communicate the meaning while including some aspects of the literal figure of speech. For example, in Ezekiel 20:5,[36] the KJV literally translated the Hebrew words "I lifted up my hand." The NASB and the ESV both replaced the original words with an interpretive restatement, "I swore." The NIV cleverly weaved both the literal figure (lifted hand) and its underlying meaning (swore) in the phrase "I swore with uplifted hand."[37] In reality, the NIV likely paints a more accurate picture of this event than any of these other versions do, since the Hebrew people generally did lift up their right hand when they uttered an oath. In this case,

---

[33] Also NLT and GW.

[34] Also HCSB.

[35] In this chart of idioms and figures of speech, it appears that at least some aspect of the NIV rendering is more literal than the KJV in two cases, more literal than the NASB in six cases and more literal than the ESV in nine cases.

[36] In twelve of the thirteen verses where this phrase occurs, the NIV included both the literal wording (lifted hand) and the underlying meaning (swore). (The only verse where the NIV left out the literal phrase "with uplifted hand" is Ezek 20:6, presumably because that phrase is explicated twice in the previous verse.) The NASB opted for a strictly interpretive rendering (swore) in all thirteen verses. The KJV used an interpretive rendering (swore) in three out of the thirteen (Ex 6:8; Num 14:30; Neh 9:15) and gave a strictly literal rendering (lifted hand) in the other ten. The ESV used a strictly interpretive rendering (swore) in eleven of the thirteen verses. In Gen 14:22, the ESV used a literal rendering (lifted hand), and in Ps 106:26, the ESV paralleled the NIV pattern of incorporating both the literal wording (lifted hand) along with the meaning (swore). The NIV is the only one of these four versions that consistently included the literal wording (lifted hand) in every context (twelve out of thirteen verses). So in the translation of this particular expression, the NIV is more literal than the NASB, ESV and KJV (also the HCSB, which closely follows the pattern of the ESV). See Gen 14:22; Ex 6:8; Num 14:30; Neh 9:15; Ps 106:26; Ezek 20:5 (twice), 6, 15, 23, 42; 36:7; 44:12; 47:14.

[37] *The Voice Bible* (VOICE) also included both the literal expression and its underlying meaning in "I lifted my hand and swore to them"; also *God's Word* (GW) translation: "I raised my hand and swore an oath."

the ESV and NASB translators again concluded that it is acceptable to interpret what the original words represent rather than reflecting the actual words.

Here are a few more examples where the NASB and/or ESV used a meaning-based rendering, but the NIV found a way to translate part of the literal phrase without sacrificing meaning (see tables 2.6, 2.7 and 2.8).

Table 2.6

Genesis 30:3	
Hebrew wording	*Be **built** from her*
NIV	***build** a family through her*
ESV	*have children through her*
NASB	*have children through her*

Table 2.7

Deuteronomy 11:10	
Hebrew wording	*water in your **foot***
NIV	*irrigated . . . **by foot***
ESV	*irrigate*

Table 2.8

Psalm 41:3	
Hebrew wording	*turn all of his **bed***
NIV	*restores them from their **bed** of illness*
NASB	*restore him to full health*
ESV	*restore him to full health*

I would like to comment on one more interesting point about Hebrew figures of speech—the KJV translation of "yoke" in 1 Samuel 14:14 (see table 2.9). Compare the translation of this verse in the following versions, noting particularly the last part of the wording in the KJV.

Table 2.9

1 Samuel 14:14	
NASB	*half a furrow in an acre of land*
NIV	*half an acre*
NKJV	*half an acre of land*
KJV	*half an acre of land, **which a yoke of oxen might plow***

Most English versions replaced the word *yoke* with "acre," but the KJV translators added an expanded, interpretive clause to their translation. They translated the Hebrew word for "yoke" as "acre . . . which a yoke of oxen might plow." I am not criticizing this expanded translation, but I find it interesting that even the King James translators waxed extremely idiomatic at times. I point this out to wonder: if the KJV made this kind of major change occasionally, is there a solid reason for saying that meaning-based versions cannot do the same thing on a more consistent basis?[38]

FIGURATIVE LANGUAGE IN GREEK

The Greek New Testament, like the Hebrew Old Testament, is rich with figurative language. Each of the Greek figures of speech in the following chart (table 2.10) was translated thought for thought rather than word for word by one or more of the versions listed. As with the previous chart, I used gray shading to mark renderings that depart significantly from the original and a white background to indicate a more literal rendering:[39]

Table 2.10

Greek Figures of Speech[a]		NASB	KJV	ESV	NIV
Mt 16:23	*Stumbling block*	Stumbling block	Offense	Hindrance	Stumbling block
Mt 18:6	*Causes . . . to stumble*	Causes . . . to stumble	Shall offend	Causes . . . to sin	Causes . . . to stumble
Mt 18:34	*Torturers*	Torturers	Tormentors	Jailers	Jailers
Mt 22:16	*Look into people's faces*[b]	Partial	Regardest . . . the person of men	Swayed by appearances	Pay . . . attention to who they are
Lk 1:34	*I do not know a man*	I am a virgin	I know not a man	I am a virgin	I am a virgin
Lk 12:35	*Loins . . . girded*	Dressed in readiness	Loins . . . girded about	Dressed for action	Dressed ready for service
Lk 15:15	*Joined himself to*	Hired himself out to	Joined himself to	Hired himself out to	Hired himself out to
Lk 20:21	*Receive a face*[c]	Are . . . partial	Acceptest . . . the person	Show . . . partiality	Show partiality

[a] Most of the Greek translations in this chart were taken from the ESV footnotes for these verses.
[b] See Grudem, "Are Only *Some* Words of Scripture Breathed Out by God?" pp. 41–42, under the heading "The Lost Faces."
[c] Ibid.

---

[38] In this verse, most English versions are more literal than the KJV.
[39] This chart is only a small sampling of Greek figures of speech used in Scripture. See also Wayne Leman, "New Testament Figures of Speech," http://bible-translation.110mb.com/ntfigures.htm, and "New Testament Idioms"; also http://betterbibles.com.

Greek Figures of Speech[a]		NASB	KJV	ESV	NIV
Jn 9:41	*Have sin*	Have . . . sin	Have . . . sin	Have . . . guilt	Be guilty of sin
Jn 13:23	*In the bosom of Jesus*	On Jesus' bosom	On Jesus' bosom	At Jesus' side	Next to him
Acts 17:24	*Made by hands*[d]	Made with hands	Made with hands	Made by man	Built by . . . hands
Rom 3:20	*Flesh*	Flesh	Flesh	Human being	One
Rom 9:16	*Runs*	Runs	Runneth	Exertion	Effort
Rom 15:28	*Sealed . . . this fruit*	Put my seal on this fruit	Sealed . . . this fruit	Delivered . . . what has been collected	Made sure . . . they . . . received this contribution
Rom 16:5	*Firstfruit*	First convert	Firstfruits	First convert	First convert
Rom 16:18	*Belly*	Appetites	Belly	Appetites	Appetites
1 Cor 1:26	*Flesh*	Flesh	Flesh	Worldly standards	Human standards
1 Cor 8:10	*Reclining at table*	Dining	Sit at meat	Eating	Eating
1 Cor 7:39	*Asleep*[e]	Dead	Dead	Dies	Dies
1 Cor 11:30		Sleep	Sleep	Died	Asleep
1 Cor 9:27	*Pummel my body and make it a slave*	Discipline my body and make it my slave	Keep under my body and bring it into subjection	Discipline my body and keep it under control	Strike a blow to my body and make it my slave
2 Cor 6:11	*Mouth . . . open*	Mouth spoken freely	Mouth . . . open	Spoken freely	Spoken freely
Gal 1:15	*From my mother's womb*	From my mother's womb	From my mother's womb	Before I was born	From my mother's womb
Phil 1:8	*bowels*	affection	bowels	affection	affection
2 Cor 7:15			inward affection		
Lk 1:78		tender [mercy]	tender [mercy]	tender [mercy]	tender [mercy]
2 Thess 3:12	*Eat their own bread*	Eat their own bread	Eat their own bread	Earn their own living	Earn the food they eat
1 Tim 1:17	*To the ages of the ages*	Forever and ever	For ever and ever	Forever and ever	For ever and ever
2 Pet 1:13	*Tent*	Earthly dwelling	Tabernacle	Body	Tent of this body
Jude 7	*Other flesh*	Strange flesh	Strange flesh	Unnatural desire	Perversion
Rev 11:8	*Spiritually*	Mystically	Spiritually	Symbolically	Figuratively

[d]Ibid., pp. 35-37, under the heading "The Missing Hands."
[e]Ibid., pp. 21-22, on the figurative use of "sleep" to signify "death."

This chart of Greek figures of speech reveals many of the same tendencies we noted in the chart of Hebrew examples. For instance, in 2 Peter 1:13, the NIV again found a way to express the metaphor's underlying meaning, "body," while at the same time reflecting part of the form, "tent." When we compare the renderings on this chart, it appears that the NIV is more literal than the KJV in Matthew 16:23, Matthew 18:6 and 1 Corinthians 9:27. Also, it is more literal than the NASB in 1 Corinthians 9:27 and 2 Peter 1:13, and more literal than the ESV in all those verses, plus three others.[40]

SHOULD THE FORM BE PRESERVED?

With any given idiom or figure of speech, we could point to specific reasons why we feel it would be beneficial to translate the actual words literally. But rather than focusing on the translation of any one figurative expression, we should look at the whole body of evidence and acknowledge the variety of methods used by translators of every English version in translating figurative language. In doing so we find that the translators of the four versions listed in these charts concluded that it is acceptable—even preferable at times—to abandon the Hebrew and Greek wording in order to faithfully and accurately translate the true meaning of biblical idioms and figures of speech.

BEYOND FIGURATIVE LANGUAGE

As we have seen, a literal translation of figurative language can often produce either wrong meaning or zero meaning[41] (i.e., nonsense). That is why idioms and figures of speech clearly illustrate the pitfalls of going too far in translating form rather than meaning. But the same principles apply with non-figurative language as well. The result may not always be wrong meaning or zero meaning, but the message will often be unclear or at least unnatural.

Throughout the rest of this book, I will quote extensively from the New American Standard Bible (NASB),[42] English Standard Version (ESV),[43] King James Version (KJV) and New King James Version (NKJV).[44] I will also quote

---

[40]Acts 17:24; 1 Cor 11:30; Gal 1:15.
[41]Cf. Beekman and Callow, *Translating the Word of God*, p. 32.
[42]NASB: www.lockman.org.
[43]ESV: www.esv.org.
[44]NKJV: www.thenkjvbible.com

from the Holman Christian Standard Bible (HCSB)[45] and the New English Translation (NET),[46] along with some others. I have tremendous appreciation for all of these versions of the Bible,[47] and I greatly respect the translators of each one. I own and regularly use each version, and I highly recommend them to every serious student of the Word. These excellent translations have made major contributions, individually and collectively, to the furtherance of the gospel and the strengthening of the church in the English-speaking world.

But what about dynamic equivalence versions (also called meaning-based or idiomatic versions) like the New International Version (NIV),[48] the New Living Translation (NLT),[49] the Contemporary English Version (CEV),[50] God's Word (GW) [51] and The Voice Bible (VOICE)?[52] What contribution do they make? Do they have value as well? What are the main differences between these various types of Bible versions? We will consider these important questions as we dig deeper into the foundations underlying the translation of God's Word into the English language.

---

[45]HCSB: www.hcsb.org.

[46]NET (also called the NET Bible): www.bible.org.

[47]As I stated in the previous chapter, I intentionally took most of the Scripture quotations in this book from literal versions in order to answer the question, Are literal versions really literal?

[48]NIV: www.biblica.com/niv.

[49]NLT: www.newlivingtranslation.com.

[50]CEV: www.americanbible.org.

[51]GW: www.godswordtranslation.org.

[52]VOICE: www.hearthevoice.com.

3

Ideal and Real

Where Theory Meets Practice

◆ ◆ ◆

Many are the plans in the mind of a man,
but it is the purpose of the LORD that will stand.

Proverbs 19:21 (ESV)

There is a proper time and procedure for every matter.

Ecclesiastes 8:6 (NET)

The English language has a long history of Bible translation, spanning several centuries. Each new English version of the Bible is unique in some ways, yet all of them share some common features. In this chapter, we will look at some of the similarities and differences between the various kinds of translations.

Cultural Ideals

Anthropologists have often used a model of cultural observation based on the ideal versus the real. The ideal describes what a person should do in a certain situation, while the real describes what a person actually does in that situation. The most notable instances of this principle playing itself out in any culture are when the real does not match the ideal.

During the years that we were studying the Lamogai culture and language, we asked the Lamogai people numerous questions about their culture. When we did, we found that most of their answers focused exclusively on the ideal. It did not take us long to realize that we needed to be careful not to form conclusions too quickly. Often, the real customs and practices that we observed in their everyday lives did not line up with what they described as their ideals. The Lamogai were not unique in this respect; this is true of people from every culture, including our own.

Here is an example from our Christian culture of a possible mismatch between an ideal and its real manifestation in our everyday lives:

- IDEAL: As a Christian, I am a picture for all the world to see, exemplifying what my heavenly Father is like: loving and kind, quick to forgive, eager to extend grace to those who do not deserve it.

- REAL: (I will let you fill in this part yourself.)

When the ideal and real in my life do not line up, which one are people most likely to believe?

IDEAL TRANSLATION STANDARDS

Most of the books and articles that have been written about Bible translation deal with the academic, theoretical side—describing the ideal standards for translation. Some authors enter the storehouse of real data only when they want to find examples that support their own ideals. It is fine to discuss ideals, but those ideals need to be held in tension by what is rooted in reality. Focusing on the ideal to the exclusion of the real would be the same as saying, "Do as I say, not as I do."

It is not my aim to resolve the academic debate of translation ideals. Others are far more qualified than I am to argue the theoretical. Instead, I would like to redirect the spotlight and approach this issue mainly from the real world of translation practice, letting the evidence speak for itself. For example, we could debate the validity of the statement "Meaning has priority over form." But what would that prove? Instead, let us look at the evidence. What have literal English versions done in practice? Have they given priority to meaning over form, or form over meaning? We will consider this and other crucial questions as we examine more of the real translation evi-

dence. But in order to properly understand the evidence at hand, we need
to first look at the various kinds of Bible versions that exist in English.

Types of Translations

Translation theorists often use a continuum like the one in figure 3.1 to describe the various types of Bible versions, ranging from more literal to less
literal. John Beekman and John Callow[1] divide this continuum into four
categories: *highly literal* translations, *modified literal* translations, *idiomatic*
translations and *unduly free* translations. They identify the translation types
at both extreme ends of the continuum (highly literal and unduly free) as
"unacceptable," and the two translation types in the middle of the continuum (modified literal and idiomatic) as "acceptable."

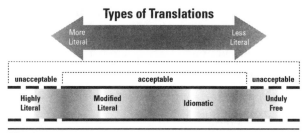

Fig. 3.1.

Highly Literal Translations

Highly literal translations do not attempt to stay within the bounds of
English grammar rules. Interlinear translations fall into this category.[2] They
focus almost exclusively on words, trying to match each Hebrew and Greek
word with a suitable English word. They also maintain the Hebrew and
Greek word order. Interlinear translations are so literal that the reader will
often find it difficult to determine the meaning of the sentence or paragraph. Here is an interlinear example of a highly literal translation of a
phrase from Lamogai:

> Lamogai: *aninom igina*
>
> English: name-your who

The highly literal English rendering "name-your who" does not commu-

---

[1]John Beekman and John Callow, *Translating the Word of God* (Grand Rapids: Zondervan,
1974), p. 21, chart 1.
[2]Ibid.

nicate any real meaning. A meaningful translation of this Lamogai phrase would be, "What is your name?"

Interlinear translations have their place as a valuable study tool—especially for those who are not familiar with the original languages. But these highly literal, interlinear translations would not be appropriate for general use. That is why Beekman and Callow classified them as "unacceptable."

Modified Literal Translations

The modified literal category in Beekman and Callow's chart includes translations that we would normally refer to as literal translations, such as the King James Version (KJV), the New American Standard Bible (NASB) and the English Standard Version (ESV). However, no translation is truly literal in the strictest sense of the term; every literal version has made many modifications. That is why Beekman and Callow used the term "modified literal" instead of "literal." Modified literal translations focus closely on words, often modifying the Hebrew and Greek grammar just enough to fit into acceptable English sentence structure.[3]

Idiomatic Translations

Idiomatic translations (also called meaning-based or dynamic-equivalence translations) focus less on finding one English word to translate each Hebrew and Greek word, and they do not try to reflect Hebrew or Greek literary style. Instead, they place higher priority on clarity and naturalness. Their goal is to clearly express the meaning of the original in a form that represents current, acceptable, English literary style. The New Living Translation (NLT), the Contemporary English Version (CEV), *God's Word* (GW) and *The Voice* (VOICE) are idiomatic translations.

Unduly Free Translations

Unduly free translations disregard basic translation principles, freely changing the meaning, historical setting and participants to suit a particular audience. The classic example of an unduly free translation in English is the *Cotton Patch Version*. Consider the following example, keeping in mind that the intended target audience is people living in the southern United States.

---

[3]Cf. Mildred L. Larson, *Meaning-Based Translation: A Guide to Cross-Language Equivalence*, rev. ed. (Lanham, MD: University Press of America, 1998), p. 18.

Acts 20:1-12 (Cotton Patch Version)[4]

> After the excitement died down, Paul called together the fellowship, and
> when he had reassured them he told them goodbye and left to go West. He
> traveled all through those parts and spoke the good word to them. Then
> he went to Texas and spent three months there. . . . In the party by now
> were Searcy Powell, a native of Akron; Stocky and Seymour from
> Cleveland; Garry and Tim from New Orleans; and Tic and Troy from
> Alabama. They all went on ahead and waited for the rest of us in St. Louis.
> After Thanksgiving we caught a bus in Houston and joined them in St.
> Louis where we stayed a week. On Sunday night we all gathered for a
> church supper, and Paul spoke. He kept going until midnight since he was
> planning to leave next day. It was hot and stuffy in the upstairs room
> where we were meeting. A young fellow named Eubanks was sitting in the
> window, and while Paul preached on and on, he dozed off and fell sound
> asleep. He was really sawing wood when all of a sudden he fell out the
> window to the ground three stories below. He was dead when we got to
> him. But Paul rushed down, knelt beside him and put his arms around
> him. "Don't y'all get upset," he said, "he's still breathing." Then Paul went
> back upstairs, fixed a sandwich and ate it, began a lengthy discussion that
> lasted till daybreak, and then left. Those in the party took the boy, Eubanks,
> home alive, and were thrilled no end about that.

It is clear to see that the translator of this passage radically changed the
historical meaning. This kind of translation is considered unduly free.

A RANGE, NOT A PRECISE POINT

There is no such thing as a purely modified literal translation or a purely
idiomatic translation. If you look at the continuum in figure 3.1, you will
notice that the lines between the different types of translations are blurred.
That is intentional, because there are no clear-cut lines of demarcation between the four types.[5] Every translation fluctuates back and forth along this
continuum—some more than others—but all translations vary in their
degree of literalness from passage to passage, verse to verse and even word

---

[4]Clarence Jordan, *The Cotton Patch Version of Luke and Acts: Jesus' Doings and Happenings*
(New York: Association Press, 1969).
[5]Cf. D. A. Carson, *The King James Version Debate: A Plea for Realism* (Grand Rapids: Baker
Book House, 1979), p. 87. Carson states, "There is . . . no indisputable step that signals the
crossing of the line from 'literal' translation to paraphrase."

to word. Although some translators have tried to assign an approximate point along this continuum for each English translation, I think it would be more appropriate, and accurate, to assign a range for each translation.

Every Bible version has two separate ranges: the ideal range and the real range. The ideal range represents the stated objectives of the translators. The real range represents the translation choices that the translators have made in each context. In figure 3.2, I have attempted to approximate the ideal and real ranges of modified literal versions.

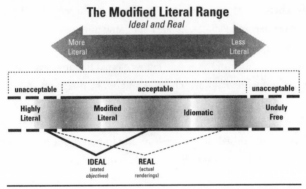

Fig. 3.2.

As this diagram indicates, all modified literal translations, including the KJV, ESV and NASB, sometimes step away from their stated translation objectives (the ideal), sliding toward the idiomatic side of this continuum to find an appropriate rendering (the real). We have already seen this demonstrated in several examples in earlier chapters.[6]

Let us look at another example: the Greek phrase "flesh and blood" (*sarx kai haima*) in Galatians 1:16. Here is how the KJV, NASB and ESV translated this phrase.

Table 3.1

Galatians 1:16	
KJV	*I conferred not with **flesh and blood***
NASB	*I did not . . . consult with **flesh and blood***
ESV	*I did not . . . consult with **anyone**[a]*

[a]Also HCSB.

---

[6]See chap. 1, tables 1.1 through 1.10; chap. 2, tables 2.5 and 2.10.

Consider how the translation of this verse applies to the ideal and real model in figure 3.3. In this case, the ESV[7] broke tradition with the essentially literal rendering "flesh and blood" and went with the highly idiomatic rendering "anyone" instead.

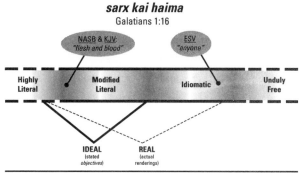

Fig. 3.3.

Of course we saw in chapter 1 that it is not always the ESV that lands on the idiomatic side of this continuum.[8] In Acts 2:17, the NASB[9] and HCSB[10] decided to slide into the idiomatic range.

Table 3.2

Acts 2:17	
ESV	*I will pour out my Spirit on all **flesh***
NASB	*I will pour forth of my Spirit on all **mankind***
HCSB	*I will pour out My Spirit on all **humanity***

From these examples, we can conclude that these versions are not consistently literal, regardless of their stated intent. We will look at many more examples which show that when we consider the real and not just the ideal, it becomes apparent that every literal version uses classic dynamic equivalence principles in many contexts. They just do

---

[7]See also the ESV's thought-for-thought translation of "flesh" in Lev 17:14; Eccles 5:6; Rom 3:20; 11:14; 1 Cor 1:26, 29; 7:28; 10:18; 2 Cor 3:3; Eph 6:5; Col 3:22; Jude 7.

[8]See chap. 1, table 1.5.

[9]See also the NASB's thought-for-thought translation of "flesh" in Lev 15:7; 20:19; Ps 65:2; Is 66:23, 24; Jer 12:12; Dan 4:12; Joel 2:28; Mt 24:22; Mk 13:20; Rom 11:14; 1 Cor 1:29; 7:28; Gal 4:14.

[10]See also the HCSB's thought-for-thought translation of "flesh" in Gen 6:3; Is 40:5; Ezek 11:19; Rom 11:14; Gal 1:16.

not do it as frequently or as consistently as the idiomatic versions do.

The translators of literal versions such as the ESV and NASB are aware of the tension that exists between ideal and real translation, and they acknowledge that tension in their Bible introductions. For example, the introduction to the ESV includes the following statement: "Every translation is at many points a trade-off between literal precision and readability, between 'formal equivalence' in expression and 'functional equivalence' in communication."[11] However, the overarching ideal of literal translations is summed up in this definitive statement about literalness (also from the ESV introduction): "an 'essentially literal' translation . . . seeks *as far as possible* to capture the precise wording of the original text and the personal style of each Bible writer."[12]

Clearly, in Galatians 1:16, the ESV did not go "as far as possible" in seeking to "capture the precise wording of the original" when the translators replaced "flesh and blood" (*sarx kai haima*) with "anyone." This is the kind of ideal that is frequently set aside by the translators of every literal version.

THE IDIOMATIC RANGE

In order to be more in line with current English literary style, idiomatic translations (figure 3.4) set their ideal target range on the idiomatic side of the continuum rather than the literal side. They aim to communicate the meaning of Scripture as clearly and naturally as possible, and for that reason, they do not place a high priority on trying to reflect the original grammatical forms.

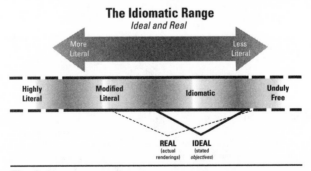

Fig. 3.4.

---

[11] English Standard Version (ESV), introduction.
[12] Ibid. (emphasis added).

WHERE DOES THE NEW INTERNATIONAL VERSION FIT?

The New International Version (NIV) is a special case and deserves to be mentioned separately. In most areas of translation, it appears that the NIV translators attempted to identify the fine line between what readers perceive to be a modified literal rendering and an idiomatic rendering.[13] They apparently set this theoretical point as the center of their target range and worked outward in both directions, depending on the constraints of each passage (figure 3.5).[14] This strategy has worked well for the NIV, which has become one of the best-selling Bibles in the English-speaking world. Gordon Fee and Mark Strauss describe this kind of version as a "mediating" translation.[15]

Fig. 3.5.

SEEKING TO BE "TRANSPARENT" TO THE ORIGINAL TEXT

Modified literal versions place a high priority on the ideal of giving a transparent[16] view into the forms of the original text—particularly the original words. Thus, when we read the words in a literal version such as the KJV, ESV or NASB it should be like looking through a "transparent" window, which would presumably give a clear view into the wording of the original. Leland

---

[13]It appears that the ideal target range of the HCSB and the NET are fairly close to that of the NIV.

[14]See Kenneth L. Barker, "Bible Translation Philosophies with Special Reference to the New International Version," in *The Challenge of Bible Translation*, ed. Glen G. Scorgie, Mark L. Strauss and Steven M. Voth (Grand Rapids: Zondervan, 2003), pp. 51-63.

[15]Gordon D. Fee and Mark L. Strauss, *How to Choose a Translation for All Its Worth* (Grand Rapids: Zondervan, 2007), p. 28.

[16]For example, the preface to the English Standard Version (ESV) includes the following statement: "[the ESV] seeks to be transparent to the original text, letting the reader see as directly as possible the structure and meaning of the original."

Ryken gives the following threefold description of what it means to be "transparent to the original text":[17]

- "Transparency to that text . . . [includes] making sure that an English reader knows what the *words of the original* are."

- [Transparency also] "requires retaining the *images and figurative language* of the Bible."

- "To be transparent to the original text means preserving *all signposts to the ancient world* of the biblical writers, as opposed to finding [modern] equivalents."

It is fine for a team of translators to establish this level of transparency as an ideal to aim for, but the real evidence shows that no translation is consistently transparent in this way. For example, in chapter 1, we saw more than one hundred instances in the NASB and ESV of thought-for-thought renderings which do not show the English reader "what the words of the original are."[18] Also, in chapter 2, we saw dozens of places where some of the most literal English versions chose not to retain "the images and figurative language" of the original—even in some verses where they could have if they had wanted to.[19] Later in the book we will examine places in Scripture where literal English versions introduced modern equivalents, rather than "preserving all signposts to the ancient world of the biblical writers."

In the next chapter, we will take a closer look at the goal of providing transparency to the original text, particularly as it relates to the words of the original. We will also contemplate some of the challenges translators have faced when attempting to translate those words faithfully and accurately into the English language.

---

[17]Ryken, *Understanding English Bible Translation*, pp. 73-74 (emphasis added).
[18]See chap. 1, tables 1.3 and 1.4.
[19]See chap. 2, tables 2.5 and 2.10.

4

What Is in a Word?

More, and Less, Than Meets the Eye

◆ ◆ ◆

Man shall not live by bread alone,
but by every word that comes from the mouth of God.

Matthew 4:4 (esv)

The unfolding of your words gives light;
it imparts understanding to the simple.

Psalm 119:130 (esv)[1]

The Building Blocks of Language

Every language is made up of many different parts that join together to form a sort of pyramid (figure 4.1) or multilevel hierarchy.[2] In this language pyramid, the units on each level are the building blocks that form the next level. The smallest unit in this pyramid is called a *morpheme*. Morphemes include prefixes, suffixes and verb roots. They join together to form words, words join together to form phrases and clauses, and sentences join into a paragraph. Paragraphs also join together to form larger units, like an episode in a story or a chapter in a book.

---

[1]This part of the verse has the same wording in the nasb and niv.
[2]Cf. Mildred L. Larson, *Meaning-Based Translation: A Guide to Cross-Language Equivalence*, rev. ed. (Lanham, MD: University Press of America, 1998), p. 33.

While there is meaning on all levels of this pyramid, for some reason we often treat the word level as though it is the most important. In this chapter, we will focus on the words of Scripture—taking special note of the way these words have been translated in literal English versions.[3] Later, in chapter 6, we will address the relationship between word-for-word translation and verbal, plenary inspiration.

Grammatical Hierarchy

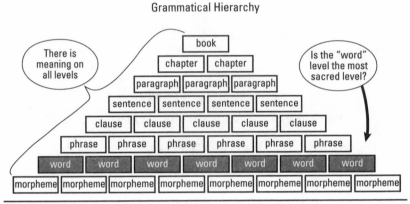

Fig. 4.1.

IS IT REALLY WORD FOR WORD?

Many Christians assume that literal versions translate each Hebrew or Greek word with a single English word. But there is no such thing as a consistent word-for-word translation of the Bible. That is because the full meaning of most words does not transfer directly between any two languages. Meaning should be viewed as an area,[4] rather than a precise point. In translating from one language to another, we usually find only partial overlap of meaning between any two "corresponding" words.[5]

For example, the Greek word *agapē* is most often translated "love" in English. But there is not precise, word-for-word correspondence, because the area of meaning of *agapē* is not identical to the area of meaning of the English word *love* (see figure 4.2). Sometimes we use "love" in contexts where *agapē* would

---

[3]Cf. Gordon D. Fee and Mark L. Strauss, *How to Choose a Translation for All Its Worth* (Grand Rapids: Zondervan, 2007), pp. 45-60.

[4]Cf. Eugene A. Nida, *Bible Translating* (London: United Bible Societies, 1947), p. 25.

[5]Cf. Mark L. Strauss, *Distorting Scripture? The Challenge of Bible Translation and Gender Accuracy* (Downers Grove, IL: InterVarsity Press, 1998), pp. 77-78.

not fit, as in the expressions "love of baseball" and "love affair." While there is quite a bit of overlap between *agapē* and "love," the overlap is not 100 percent.

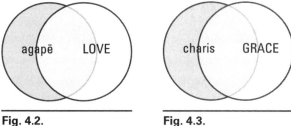

Fig. 4.2.   **Fig. 4.3.**

Another example is the Greek word *charis* (figure 4.3), which is translated "grace" nearly 130 times in the KJV. Does faithfulness in translation require translators to do a word-for-word translation of the word *charis*, translating it "grace" in every instance? No. I do not know of any Bible version that has done that.

The Greek word *charis* occurs 155 times in the New Testament. The King James translators exchanged this Greek noun for an English verb four times,[6] and three times they exchanged it for an adjective.[7] Where they translated *charis* as a noun, they translated it seven different ways other than "grace" (table 4.1).

Table 4.1

χάρις (*charis*) in the KJV			
Verbs	**Adjectives**	**Nouns**	
thank	acceptable	benefit	joy
be thanked	gracious	favour	liberality
	thankworthy	gift	pleasure
		grace	thanks

For the vast majority of readers, this sundry assortment of vaguely related English words would not give a transparent view into the original text. In fact, most readers would have no idea that all these words represent the standard Greek word for "grace" (*charis*).

---

[6]Lk 17:9; Rom 6:17; 1 Tim 1:12; 2 Tim 1:3.
[7]Lk 4:22; 1 Pet 2:19, 20.

Is a Word Always a Word?

As we consider the importance of words in the New Testament, it would be fitting to examine the Greek word *logos*, since this term is most often translated "word" in our English versions.

If I were to ask you what *logos* means, you would probably say it means "word." But that is only partially correct. "Word" is the most common way to translate *logos* into English, but it is not the only way. The KJV translated *logos* twenty-four different ways. Here is a list of the KJV renderings of *logos* (table 4.2).

Table 4.2

λόγος *(logos)* in the KJV			
account	matter	rumour	thing
cause	mouth	say	tidings
communication	move	sayings	treatise
doctrine	preaching	speech	utterance
fame	question	shew	word
intent	reason	talk	work

The word *logos* occurs inconspicuously in some very familiar verses. The average reader of the KJV may be surprised to learn the various places where *logos* is used. The following chart (table 4.3) lists several occurrences of *logos* in the King James New Testament. The words used by the KJV to translate *logos* in each of these contexts are included in parentheses underneath the word *logos*.

Table 4.3

λόγος *(logos)* in the KJV	
Acts 1:1	The former *logos* have I made, O Theophilus (treatise)
Rom 14:12	So then every one of us shall give *logos* of himself to God. (account)
1 Cor 1:18	For the *logos* of the cross is to them that perish foolishness (preaching)
1 Cor 2:1	[I] came not with excellency of *logos* (speech)
1 Cor 2:4	my *logos* and my preaching [were] not with enticing words (speech)
Eph 4:29	Let no corrupt *logos* proceed out of your mouth (communication)
1 Tim 1:15	This [is] a faithful *logos* and worthy of all acceptation (saying)

λόγος *(logos)* in the KJV	
1 Pet 3:15	[be] ready always to [give] an answer to every man that asketh you a ***logos*** of the hope that is in you (reason)
Acts 20:24	But *of no **logos***, neither count I my life dear unto myself (none of these things move me)
Mt 5:32	whosoever shall put away his wife, saving for the ***logos*** of fornication (cause)

Yes, sometimes *logos* does mean "word." But in the KJV we find that it also means "treatise," "account," "reason," "communication" and "saying," among the twenty-four possibilities. Many of the twenty-four renderings of *logos* in the KJV are used in other versions too, such as the ESV and NASB. But those versions also translated *logos* in ways that the KJV did not. If we survey all the ways the ESV and NASB translated *logos*, we will find more than thirty additional renderings. Here are several examples (table 4.4).

Table 4.4

More Renderings of *logos* (from the ESV and NASB)			
answer	ground	retort	teaching
appearance	justify	sentence	testimony
book	message	speaking	that
complaint	news	statement	what (was spoken)
conversation	remark	story	why
credit	report	talking	word of mouth

In these three English versions alone, the Greek word *logos* is translated more than fifty different ways! So back to our original question: Is a word always a word? Apparently not. If we apply the translation model introduced in chapter 2 to the word *logos*, it could look something like figure 4.4.

It is clear by this illustration that the area of meaning of the Greek word *logos* is much broader than the area of meaning of "word" in English. There is some overlap, but it is not 100 percent.

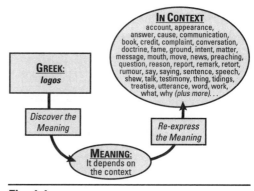

Fig. 4.4.

Logos: More Than Just a Word

The most basic meaning of "word" in English is the smallest grammatical unit that can stand alone. There are some places in Scripture where the Greek word *logos* refers to this kind of grammatical word; one example is in 1 Corinthians 14:19 (HCSB): "in the church I would rather speak five words (Gk *logos*) with my understanding, in order to teach others also, than 10,000 words in [another] language." In this context, *logos* represents a single word. But that is not the case in most contexts. *Logos* often refers to a statement or a message on the phrase, clause or sentence level—or even on higher levels, like a paragraph or book.[8] Yet "word" has become the default rendering of *logos* in most English versions. In many situations, that rendering works fine because "word" in English can be used in a broad sense just like *logos*. But closer examination shows that "word" may not always be the best way to translate *logos*.

Sometimes in our English versions, it sounds as though *logos* is referring to a single word, even though the context is clearly talking about a larger unit, like a phrase or a sentence. For example, Galatians 5:14 is translated this way in the ESV: "For the whole law is fulfilled in one word (Gk *logos*): 'You shall love your neighbor as yourself.'" In English this sounds a bit peculiar, because the command in this verse ("You shall love your neighbor as yourself") is not just "one word," as the verse indicates; it is seven (six in Greek) and is a grammatical sentence. So in this case, it may be better not to use the standard English rendering "word," since this verse is obviously talking about a statement made up of several words. The Holman Christian Standard Bible (HCSB) translated *logos* as "statement" rather than "word" in this verse: "For the entire law is fulfilled in one statement: You shall love your neighbor as yourself."

The term "statement" falls well within the boundaries of the area of meaning of *logos*. It would have been possible for the ESV to use "statement" here too, since the ESV translated *logos* as "statement" in some other contexts: "he said to her, 'For this statement (Gk *logos*) you may go your way; the demon has left your daughter'" (Mk 7:29) and "When Pilate heard this statement (Gk *logos*), he was even more afraid" (Jn 19:8).

---

[8]The ESV, NIV and NLT (plus others) translated *logos* as "book" in Acts 1:1.

The NASB translators took a slightly different approach. Realizing that "word" by itself in Galatians 5:14 could be confusing, they decided to make the meaning a bit clearer by adding the word *statement* along with "word": "For the whole Law is fulfilled in one word, in the statement, 'You shall love your neighbor as yourself'" (Gal 5:14).

The KJV, like the ESV, translated *logos* as "word" in Galatians 5:14. Is "word" a more accurate translation of *logos* than "statement" or "saying"? I do not believe it is. I believe "statement" or "saying" would be just as accurate as "word" in this context. This is confirmed by the fact that the KJV translated *logos* as "saying" in the very closely related parallel verse, Romans 13:9: "if [there be] any other commandment, it is briefly comprehended in this saying (Gk *logos*), namely, Thou shalt love thy neighbour as thyself."

There is no difference between Galatians 5:14 and Romans 13:9 that would make it necessary to translate *logos* as "word" in one case and "saying" in the other. The point of these two verses is identical. So why did the KJV translate them differently? Was it an oversight? In fact, this issue is older than the KJV.

When John Wycliffe translated the Scriptures into English in the fourteenth century, he translated *logos* as "word" in both of these verses. About 150 years later, when William Tyndale produced his translation, he must have noticed the apparent contradiction in Romans 13:9 in describing the six-word command *Love thyne neghbour as thy selfe* as a single "word." So he translated it "sayinge" rather than "word": "yf there be eny other commaundement they are all comprehended in this sayinge (Gk *logos*): Love thyne neghbour as thy selfe."[9]

For some reason Tyndale did not make this change in Galatians 5:14. He kept the rendering "word" from Wycliffe's translation. There is no way to know for sure why he changed it in Romans and not in Galatians, but we should remember that all translators are human. I am a translator myself, so I know how much of a challenge it can be to achieve total consistency between all parallel passages—especially without a computer!

I find it interesting that in Romans 13:9, the vast majority of English versions followed the pattern set by William Tyndale in the sixteenth century;

---

[9]Tyndale New Testament, Worms Octavo Edition.

they translated *logos* as "saying" (or something similar), rather than "word."[10] This is just one example which shows that many translational choices in English are based more on tradition than on actual wording differences in the original.

WHAT IS THE PRIMARY MEANING?

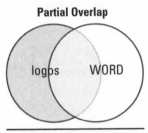

Partial Overlap

logos   WORD

Fig. 4.5.

Since *logos* has been translated so many different ways in English, why was it decided that "word" should be its default rendering? Was it because "word" is the primary meaning of *logos*? Not necessarily. James Strong, in the *Greek Dictionary of the New Testament*,[11] does not include "word" in his definition of *logos*:

logos *log´-os*; something said (including the thought); by implication, a topic (subject of discourse), also reasoning (the mental faculty) or motive; by extension, a computation; specially, (with the article in John) the Divine Expression (i.e. Christ).[12]

If "word" is not necessarily the primary meaning of the Greek word *logos*, then how did it become the predominant English rendering?

FINDING THE "DEFAULT" RENDERING

When the earliest translators chose "word" to be the most common English translation for *logos*, it was based on area of meaning. There is quite a bit of overlap between *logos* and "word," even though the overlap is only partial (figure 4.5). In fact, all fifty of the English renderings[13] for *logos* in the KJV, ESV and NASB share some overlap of meaning with *logos*. The word *account*, for example, is used by all three of these versions to translate *logos* in some contexts. But the area of meaning of "account" overlaps only slightly with the area of

---

[10]The ESV is one of very few English versions that translated *logos* as "word" in Rom 13:9.

[11]James Strong, "Greek Dictionary of the New Testament," in *The Exhaustive Concordance of the Bible* (New York: Abingdon, 1890).

[12]Strong lists several ways *logos* is translated in the KJV, including "word," but "word" does not appear in his definition of *logos*. Some other lexicons do include "word" in their definition of *logos*.

[13]See chap. 4, tables 4.2, 4.3, 4.4 and figure 4.4.

meaning of *logos* (see figure 4.6). The word *speech* has a bit more in common with *logos* than "account" does, but no English term seems to have as much in common with *logos* as "word." Based on its area of meaning overlap, literal versions have chosen "word" as the default term for translating *logos*.

How Do You Translate a Word?

When a translator considers how to translate a particular Greek or Hebrew word into English, there are two basic approaches:

1. Try to match the area of meaning of that word in all its occurrences.

2. Try to match the specific meaning of that word in each individual context.

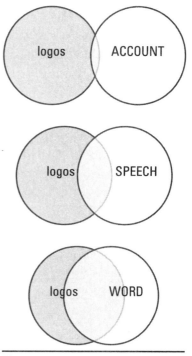

Fig. 4.6.

These approaches highlight a key difference between the way words are translated in literal versions and idiomatic versions. Literal versions usually adopt the first of these two approaches as their ideal, matching the area of meaning of each word whenever it is practical to do so. Idiomatic versions usually adopt the second approach. Their first priority is to match the specific meaning of each word depending on the context.

Since literal versions give greater weight to the area of meaning, they usually consider "word" to be the best overall choice for translating *logos*. But since idiomatic versions give greater weight to the specific meaning in each context, they usually consider "word" to be just one valid choice among many.

Even though the translators of literal versions prefer to translate *logos* as "word," they realize this is just an ideal to aim for. Out of the 330 occurrences of *logos* in the New Testament, the KJV, ESV and NASB each set aside this ideal about a hundred times. Even the highly word-focused *Young's Literal Translation* (YLT) set aside this ideal forty-five times. Every time the translators of a literal version translated *logos* as something other than "word," they were allowing the context to determine the meaning. This shows that literal versions do not discount the context—they just do not give it as much priority as idiomatic versions do.

Every English version translated *logos* as "word" in some contexts, but no version translated it "word" every time (see figure 4.7). *Young's Literal Translation* (YLT) translated *logos* as "word" 86% of the time. The other 14% of the time, *logos* was translated in other ways. The rest of the versions (see figure 4.7) were willing to set aside the default rendering "word" much more often. If "word" is the most accurate way to translate *logos*, then the NASB and ESV achieved only about 70% accuracy and the KJV achieved only 66%.

Logos as "word"	Other Renderings		
YLT	word	86%	14%
NASB	word	72%	28% (other)
ESV	word	70%	30% (other)
KJV	word	66%	34% (other)
NIV	word	54%	46% (other)
NET	word	53%	47% (other)
HCSB	word	45%	55% (other)
NLT	word	27%	73% (other)

Fig. 4.7.

ADDING AND TAKING AWAY

One of the most solemn warnings in the entire Bible is found in Revelation 22:18-19. Every translator needs to take the warning of these verses seriously:

> I testify to everyone who hears the words (Gk *logos*) of the prophecy of this book: if anyone adds to them, God will add to him the plagues which are written in this book; and if anyone takes away from the words (Gk *logos*) of the book of this prophecy, God will take away his part from the tree of life and from the holy city, which are written in this book.[14]

What does this passage mean when it warns not to "take away from the words (*logos*) of the book of this prophecy"? Are these verses saying that

---

[14]Rev 22:18-19 (NASB).

every Greek word needs to be represented in every translation by an English word? Or a Lamogai word?

There are a number of occurrences of *logos* in the Greek New Testament that are not represented by any word at all in some English versions. In the following examples (table 4.5), I inserted the standard rendering "word" each time *logos* appears in the Greek text of these verses. Look carefully at the KJV translation of these verses and compare it with the Greek wording.

Table 4.5

	King James Version	Greek
Mt 25:19	reckoneth with them	reckons **words** with them
1 Cor 15:2	keep in memory what I preached unto you	hold fast what **word** I preached to you
Phil 4:15	no church communicated with me as concerning giving and receiving	not one church shared with me in **word** of expenses and receipts
Heb 4:13	of him with whom we have to do	of him to whom [is] our **word**

In each of these verses, it may appear that the King James translators "took away" from the *logos* of Scripture—in a most literal sense! Did they disregard the warning of Revelation 22:19? I do not believe they did. If you look closely at these verses, you will find that although the KJV omitted the word *logos*, nothing is missing from the original meaning.

COUNTING WORDS

What does the warning in Revelation 22:18-19 mean? Are these verses saying we should do a word count of our English Bible versions to find out how faithful they are to the original? If that is the case, every English version is in trouble. To illustrate this point, let us count the number of words in Revelation 22:18-19 in several English versions.

When you look at the chart (table 4.6), you may be surprised to see which versions added the most words. Of course, the comparative word count in Greek depends on which Greek text you use.[15] If the warning in Revelation 22:18-19 was suggesting an actual word count, then it could be

---

[15]Most of the differences between the Scrivener (Textus Receptus) and UBS (Critical Text) readings of these two verses are so minor that they do not show up in our English translations. The only noticeable difference is "book of life" (Scrivener) contrasted with "tree of life" (UBS) in Rev 22:19, but that does not affect the word count.

said that the KJV added twenty words to the text! (Go ahead—count them for yourself.) But I do not believe those twenty additional words in the KJV add anything to the meaning. The King James translators knew that increasing the number of words (even by 30% in this case) did not change the God-breathed message of Scripture.

Table 4.6

Revelation 22:18-19[a] Word Count[b]	
Greek (Scrivener[c]) =	61 words
Greek (UBS[d]) =	65 words
HCSB =	61 words
ESV =	65 words[e]
NIV =	67 words
NASB =	68 words
NLT =	68 words
YLT =	80 words
KJV =	81 words

plus 20 words

[a] This comparison is adapted and expanded from a similar example presented by Scott Munger (Biblica) at an academic forum for Bible translation called "Bible Translation 2001," held at the Graduate Institute of Applied Linguistics (Dallas, TX, October 2001).

[b] Rev 22:18-19 word count for a few more versions: CEV 60; GW 64; NRSV 66; NET 67; NCV and PHILLIPS 70; TEV 71.

[c] F. H. A. Scrivener, *The New Testament in the Original Greek according to the Text followed in the Authorised Version* (Cambridge: Cambridge University Press, 1894, 1902).

[d] *UBS Greek New Testament*, 4th rev. ed. (Stuttgart: Deutsche Bibelgesellschaft, 1994).

[e] Even though the ESV has the same number of words as the Greek text (65), the individual words do not line up one to one between Greek and English. In these two verses, the ESV, like all the rest of these versions, has omitted some Greek words and added some English words. Coincidentally, the totals happen to be 65.

In the example above, most of the versions listed have more words than the Greek text does. But it does not always work that way. An interesting case is the genealogy in Matthew 1:1-16. In these sixteen verses, the Greek text (UBS) has 246 words. (There are 248 in the Textus Receptus.) Figure 4.8 shows that the ESV and NASB used many more words than the Greek text does; and the KJV and NKJV used considerably fewer words.

If a simple word count were the barometer, the conclusion would be that the ESV added

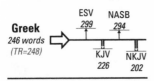

Matthew 1:1-16

Fig. 4.8.

53 words and the NASB added 48. Also, the KJV subtracted 22 words, and the NKJV subtracted 46. Ironically, all four of these versions have been described as word-for-word translations, yet the differences between them are huge. The translation of these sixteen verses in the ESV includes 97 more words than the same verses in the NKJV!

The examples in this chapter clearly show that no English Bible version is a consistent word-for-word representation of the original. The translators of every literal version have frequently set aside their ideal of transparently reflecting the original words in order to faithfully reproduce the original meaning.

THE *LOGOS*: THE LIVING WORD

The *Logos* of God is his message to humanity. But this message is more than just symbols written with ink on a page, separated by spaces and punctuation. God wanted to make sure you and I truly grasped the depth of his message to us, so he came and lived on earth as a man, personifying the flawless truths of his written word. Jesus Christ is himself the *Logos*, the living manifestation of God's eternal truth. He is God in human form:

> In the beginning was the Word, and the Word was with God, and the Word was God. . . . And the Word was made flesh, and dwelt among us.[16]

> He is clothed with a robe dipped in blood, and His name is called The Word of God.[17]

When Jesus Christ, the true *Logos*, came to earth, he did not just tell us what God is like; he showed us. This is how he explained it to his disciples:

> Anyone who has seen me has seen the Father. How can you say, "Show us the Father"? Don't you believe that I am in the Father, and that the Father is in me? The words I say to you are not just my own. Rather, it is the Father, living in me, who is doing his work.[18]

God went to great lengths to deliver his message to us in person. This message is eternal; it predates, and will outlast, all forms of human communication. As a translator, I am humbled by the profound responsibility of faithfully reflecting the living *Logos* in human language. And I am con-

---

[16]Jn 1:1, 14b (KJV).
[17]Rev 19:13 (NASB).
[18]Jn 14:9b-10 (NIV).

stantly reminded of my utter dependence on the Lord—particularly in light
of the fact that consistent, word-for-word translation of the original is not
an attainable goal in English or in any other language.

SOME TECHNICAL EXAMPLES

In the next several chapters, we will look at many more translation examples,
mainly from English and Lamogai. Most of these examples are straightforward; but some of them may seem slightly technical. If you are not linguistically inclined, please do not get bogged down by the technical nature
of some of the examples. I am including each of them to highlight the fact
that human language is extremely complex and diverse and to show that
Bible translation is a complicated process. Through these examples, I hope
to illustrate that we cannot afford to hold an oversimplified view of language and translation because oversimplification of complex issues is often
at the root of misunderstanding and disunity.

5

CRITERIA FOR ADJUSTMENT

INTENTIONALITY SAFEGUARDS THE MESSAGE

◆ ◆ ◆

Everything should be done in a fitting and orderly way.

1 CORINTHIANS 14:40 (NIV)

We have seen in previous chapters that the pursuit of faithfulness and accuracy in translation sometimes requires every translator to set aside some of the forms of the original text, rather than reflecting them literally. In this chapter, we will look at the benchmarks translators have used to decide when it is allowable, or even necessary, to set aside those original forms.

FOUR KEY CONSTRAINTS

There are four basic reasons why translators make adjustments in their translation, causing a verse or passage of Scripture to reflect less of the original form:[1]

1. Adjustment is often required by the grammar of the target language.

2. Adjustment is often needed to make sure the correct meaning comes through.

---

[1] Cf. John Beekman and John Callow, *Translating the Word of God* (Grand Rapids: Zondervan, 1974), pp. 34, 39-43, 58-62. See also Gordon D. Fee and Mark L. Strauss, *How to Choose a Translation for All Its Worth* (Grand Rapids: Zondervan, 2007), pp. 36-41.

3. Adjustment is often needed for clarity of meaning.

4. Adjustment is often necessary for the sake of naturalness.

These four criteria affect all translations in every language, including English. The specific ways that they are applied differ from translation to translation, but the translators of every version have made adjustments based on each of these criteria.

Required by the Grammar

Translators would agree that when the Bible is translated into English or any other language, it needs to be grammatically correct. The translators of every English version have taken steps to make sure their translations reflect English grammar, not Hebrew and Greek grammar.[2] Ancient Hebrew and New Testament Greek contain grammatical features that do not exist in English. Likewise, English contains features that do not exist in Hebrew or Greek. These differences have made it impossible for translators to be consistently literal at this level.

Therefore it should be no surprise that the grammar rules of English often require translators to add words that have no direct counterpart in the original and to leave out words or parts of words that are untranslatable. This is true of all translations, even the most literal ones. This reality calls for a parallel axiom to the one we already mentioned—that grammatical correctness has priority over literalness of form.

Required[3] for Correct Meaning

Grammar is not the only reason for making adjustments in translation. For example, it would be fine, from a grammatical standpoint, to translate the Hebrew phrases "in my autumn days" and "mouth of the sword"[4] literally into English. But the translators of every English version decided to change the wording of these expressions. They did not make these changes because

---

[2]The exception is with interlinear translations. See chap. 3, "Highly Literal Translations."
[3]With points 2 through 4 (correct meaning, clarity of meaning and stylistic naturalness) the question of whether or not a particular adjustment is required is a judgment call on the part of the translators. Often, some translations will make an adjustment, while others choose not to. For example, in Gal 1:16, the ESV changed "flesh and blood" to "anyone" (presumably for the sake of clarity and/or naturalness) even though many other versions did not. See table 3.1 and figure 3.3.
[4]See chap. 2, "'Autumn Days': An Example from Hebrew" and "The Edge of the Sword."

of English grammar, but rather to to communicate the correct intended meaning. This lends solid support to the axiom mentioned earlier: Meaning has priority over form.

Required for Clarity of Meaning

Faithfulness in translation goes beyond providing the bare minimum necessary to allow the correct meaning to squeak through. Translators of every English version have made frequent adjustments to make sure that the meaning is not only correct but also clearly understood by the target audience.

Required for Stylistic Naturalness

Naturalness in translation is sometimes called readability. When translators make adjustments for the sake of naturalness, they do so in order to make the translation sound more like the way we speak English. Commenting on this feature of translation, Beekman and Callow[5] suggest that "a translation should not sound like a translation at all."[6]

It is true that dynamic equivalence versions place a higher priority on naturalness and readability than literal versions do, but literal versions do not ignore naturalness as a factor in translation. Some of them include readability as one of their stated goals. For example, the preface to the English Standard Version (ESV) says, "Every translation is at many points a trade-off between literal precision and readability . . . and the ESV is no exception."[7] All English versions, including literal ones, have made many adjustments based purely on naturalness and style. We will look at some examples of this later in this chapter.

ANALYZING TRANSLATIONAL ADJUSTMENTS

There are many different ways to describe translation. I do not want to oversimplify the matter, because translation is an extremely complex undertaking. The flowchart in figure 5.1 represents one possible way of describing the translation process. The steps in this flowchart illustrate the four criteria for adjustment discussed in this chapter.

---

[5]Beekman and Callow, *Translating the Word of God*, p. 41.
[6]Some translators may say this statement pushes the pursuit of naturalness farther than it should.
[7]Also the updated NASB (1995), title page, includes the following statement: "The Most Literal Is Now More Readable."

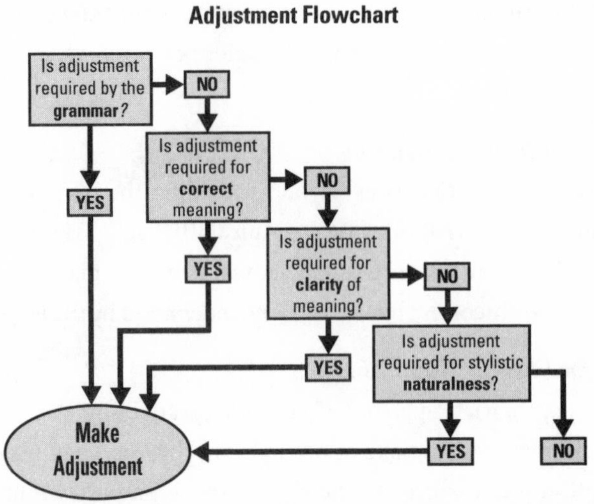

Adjustment Flowchart

Fig. 5.1.

This flowchart does not represent a new, proposed model for doing translation, nor does it apply only to dynamic equivalence versions. It illustrates a
basic translation process that has been implemented in various ways by the
translators of every English version ever produced. This will be clearly demonstrated by the examples in this chapter and throughout the rest of the book.

We will test the flowchart in figure 5.1 against an example from Scripture,
but first, I would like to comment briefly on explicit information and implicit information. The connection between these two elements of communication plays an important role in the translation decisions that are based
on the four criteria for adjustment.

Explicit and Implicit Information

All communication includes both explicit and implicit information.[8]

- Explicit information is the part of the communication that is plainly
  stated in grammatical forms (words, phrases, etc.).

- Implicit information is not represented by any actual language form.

---

[8]Cf. Mildred L. Larson, *Meaning-Based Translation: A Guide to Cross-Language Equivalence*,
rev. ed. (Lanham, MD: University Press of America, 1998), pp. 41-50; Beekman and Callow
Translating the Word of God, pp. 45-66.

However, it is information that is indeed part of the total communication intended by the writer or speaker.

Consider the example in figure 5.2.

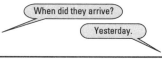

Fig. 5.2.

What does the word *yesterday* mean in this context? We know that the full meaning is "They arrived yesterday." If we translate this conversation into another language and explicitly state, "They arrived yesterday," have we added to the meaning? No, not at all. In fact, in some languages, if we do not explicitly include this information, we could be leaving out part of the original intended meaning.

Look at the next example (figure 5.3). In this context, the two-word phrase "an apple" means "I ate an apple for lunch," and the single word *red* means "The apple I ate for lunch was red." The actual form is only one word (*red*); but the complete meaning is best communicated using eight words: "The apple I ate for lunch was red." Seven out of these eight words are not explicitly represented by any actual language form, but they are definitely included in the full meaning intended by the speaker.

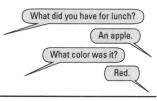

Fig. 5.3.

Here are two examples of places where the ESV, NASB and HCSB added implicit information.

Table 5.1

1 Chronicles 15:1	
Hebrew	*He built houses for himself*
ESV	*David built houses for himself*
NASB	*David built houses for himself*
HCSB	*David built houses for himself*

Table 5.2

Jeremiah 33:2	
Hebrew	*Thus says the Lord who made it*
ESV	*Thus says the Lord who made the earth*
NASB	*Thus says the Lord who made the earth*
HCSB	*The Lord who made the earth . . . says this:*

A careful translator will not arbitrarily turn implicit information into explicit information. Translators should only add implicit information when it is required by one of the four criteria for adjustment.[9]

APPLYING THE FLOWCHART TO SCRIPTURE

Let us look at how the adjustment flowchart (figure 5.1) applies to a verse of Scripture. Throughout this book, we will see many scriptural examples that illustrate the principles of this flowchart. At this point, we will look at a single phrase—the last half of Matthew 1:6. It has just nine words[10] in Greek.[11] This phrase is neither linguistically nor doctrinally complex, but from a translation standpoint, there is more here than meets the eye. The NASB translated it like this: "David was the father of Solomon by Bathsheba who had been the wife of Uriah."

The NASB has been called a "strictly literal translation."[12] Yet the NASB translators made several significant adjustments in their translation of this short, uncomplicated Greek phrase. We will consider six ways that the NASB departed from the wording of the Greek text, noting how the adjustment flowchart applies to each one.

Adjustment 1: The Word "Wife" Was Added

The word *wife* is not in the Greek text. It is implicit information that was added by the NASB translators. The Greek wording of this part of the phrase says, "David fathered Solomon by *the* of Uriah."[13] Obviously, it would not make sense in English to say "*the* of Uriah." The reader would wonder, "The *what* of Uriah?" Greek uses the feminine article (*tēs*),[14] so we know that the "the" here must refer to something feminine. That is why nearly every English version added the word *wife*.[15] Did the translators go

---

[9]See chap. 5, "Four Key Constraints."

[10]The Textus Receptus reading of this sentence has eleven words. It repeats the two words "the king" (describing David) from the first part of the verse. This minor difference does not affect any of the translational adjustments we will be highlighting here.

[11]Gk Δαυὶδ δὲ ἐγέννησεν τὸν Σολομῶνα ἐκ τῆς τοῦ Οὐρίου.
    Lit *David and fathered the Solomon by the (her) of-the of-Uriah.*

[12]www.esv.org, "How is the ESV Different from Other Translations?" This page has been removed from the most current version of the ESV website, but copies are available.

[13]This could be translated "her of Uriah."

[14]Every occurrence of the definite article (*the*) in Greek is masculine, feminine or neuter.

[15]The New Living Translation (NLT) added the word *widow* instead of wife. That is not necessarily wrong, because the Greek does not say either "wife" or "widow." Solomon's mother was both.

too far? No. Even though they added the word *wife* to the original form, they did not add anything to the original meaning.

How does the flowchart apply to this example? We will start by asking the first question: Is the addition of the word *wife* required by the grammar? The answer is yes. Therefore, we do not need to go any further on our flowchart. The obvious conclusion is that adjustment must be made (figure 5.4).

Adjustment Flowchart

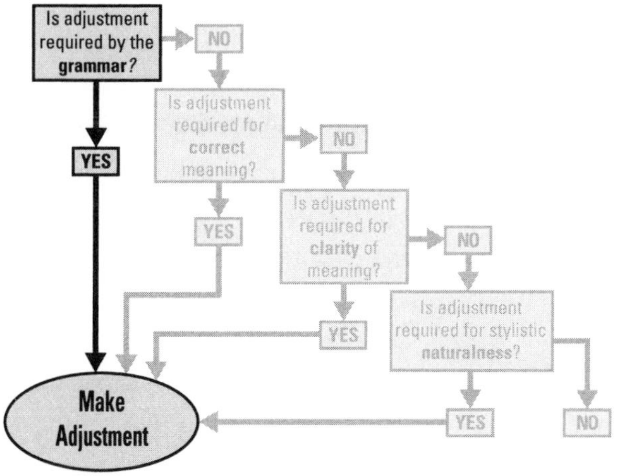

Fig. 5.4.

Adjustment 2: *The Word "the" Was Omitted (Twice)*

Greek often uses the definite article *the* in places where it cannot be translated literally into English. There are two examples of this in this phrase—just before the names Solomon and Uriah. In Greek, it reads like this: "David fathered *the* Solomon by the [wife] of *the* Uriah." Obviously, these two occurrences of the word *the* must be omitted in English because English does not use the definite article in this way. Looking again at our flowchart (figure 5.4), we see that this adjustment is also required by the grammar.

Comparing this verse with the historical context (2 Sam 11–12), we can see that there is more implied here than just the word *wife*. That does not necessarily mean that all of the implicit information has to be stated explicitly in the translation. As illustrated in adjustments 3 through 6 below, every translator needs to consider how much information is necessary for the sake of meaning, clarity or naturalness.

Adjustment 3: The Phrase "Who Had Been" Was Added

When the NASB translators added the word *wife* in this verse, they also included an extra three-word phrase, "who had been." These three words are not in the original. The NASB translation of this part of the phrase reads like this: "*who had been* the *wife* of Uriah." The translators realized that if they added the word *wife* by itself, that could be understood to mean that Bathsheba was still Uriah's wife at the time David fathered Solomon. That would mean Solomon was conceived in an adulterous relationship. We know that is not true. The baby who was conceived in adultery died shortly after he was born (2 Sam 12:18). When David fathered Solomon, Bathsheba had previously been Uriah's wife, but she was not his wife at that time because Uriah was already dead. Many English versions made this clear by adding an extra phrase not in the original. Here are some examples.

Table 5.3

NASB	**who had been** the *wife of Uriah*
KJV	*her* **that had been** *the wife of Uriah*
NKJV	*her* **who had been** *the wife of Uriah*
NIV	*whose mother* **had been** *Uriah's wife*

Let us apply the adjustment flowchart to the addition of the phrase "who had been" (figure 5.5). First, is it required by the grammar? No. It would be perfectly fine from a grammatical standpoint to leave it out. Second, is it required for correct meaning? Maybe. That depends on how familiar the reader is with the historical context. Third, is it required for clarity of meaning?

The translators of many English versions, including the NASB, apparently answered yes to this question and adjusted the verse by adding the phrase "who had been."

When the NASB translators added this phrase, they were translating the intent of the author, not his literal words. There is nothing in the original form of this verse to indicate that Solomon's mother had previously been Uriah's wife and no longer was. That information is based on the translators' knowledge of the historical account in 2 Samuel 11–12. This is a classic example of prioritizing meaning-based translation over form-based translation. In this case, the translators of several versions that are generally considered form-based decided to add these extra words to make sure the meaning was clear.[16]

Adjustment Flowchart

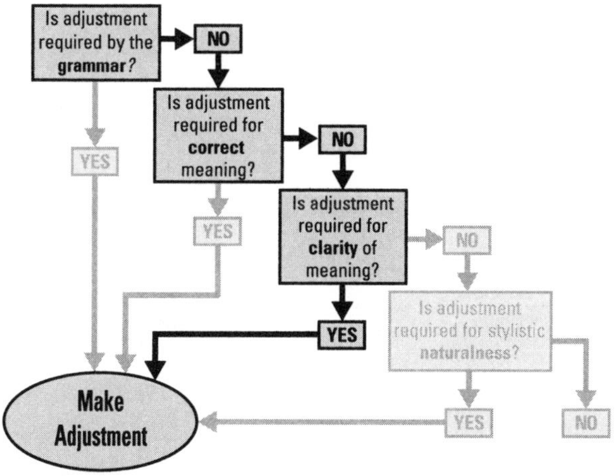

Fig. 5.5.

Adjustment 4: *The Name* Bathsheba *Was Added*[17]

Another addition made by the NASB translators is the name Bathsheba. It is not in the original. In this case, the NASB is in the minority since most English versions did not add "Bathsheba" here. Obviously, the NASB translators had good reasons for adding Bathsheba's name. Let us see how our flowchart applies to this addition (figure 5.6). Is it required by the grammar? No. What about correctness or clarity of meaning? Probably not. No one disputes who Solomon's mother was. Bathsheba is clearly identified as the mother of Solomon at least three times in Scripture.[18] That leaves only one apparent reason for this adjustment: increased naturalness.

---

[16]Even though the NASB, KJV and others added this extra phrase, some versions, such as the ESV and HCSB, determined that it was unnecessary. This reflects a judgment call on the part of the translators of these versions.

[17]The name Bathsheba is not in earlier editions of the NASB. It was added in a later, updated edition.

[18]2 Sam 12:24; 1 Kings 1:11; 2:13.

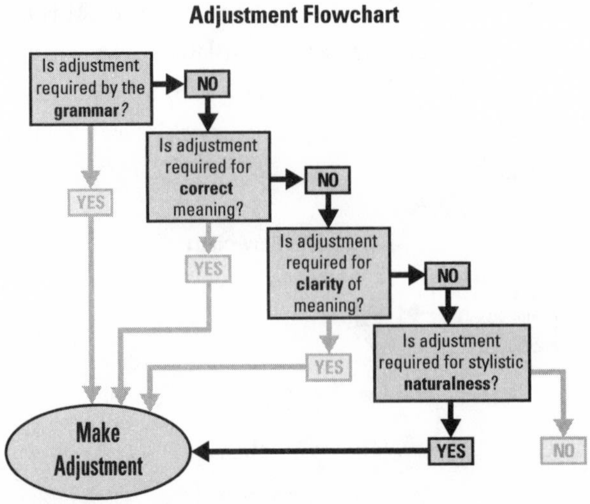

Adjustment Flowchart

Fig. 5.6.

Here are two likely explanations of why the NASB translators added the name Bathsheba in this verse:

- In Greek, every person in the genealogical thread of this passage is mentioned by name except Bathsheba.[19] The decision by the NASB translators to include Bathsheba's name follows the pattern of the rest of the passage.

- Also, in English it may be more natural to add her name than it would be to leave it out. It is usually considered proper to refer to people by name when possible, rather than indirectly.

The name Bathsheba does not occur anywhere in the Greek New Testament, but it does occur in the NASB translation of Matthew 1:6. Did the NASB translators inappropriately add to Scripture? I do not believe they did. It is true that they added an extra word that is not in the original, but they did not add anything to the meaning of the verse. They concluded that it was appropriate to add the name Bathsheba for the sake of naturalness (and perhaps clarity). After all, she is definitely the person this verse is talking about. Obviously, the NASB translators

---

[19]The only other individuals in this passage who are not mentioned by name are Judah's brothers (Mt 1:2) and Jeconiah's brothers (Mt 1:11). These two groups of brothers are peripheral in this context because they are not members of the genealogical thread through which Christ's lineage is traced.

felt that adding the name Bathsheba does not violate the warning of Revelation 22:18.[20]

In this verse, the NASB added four consecutive words that are not in the original: "Bathsheba who had been."[21] The NASB translators concluded, at least in this case, that it is acceptable for translators to add words or phrases that may be implied from the historical context even if those words are not included in the original text.

Careful examination of even the most literal English versions will expose many occurrences like this where the translators waxed idiomatic, so to speak. In this case, the NIV is more literal than the NASB as it chose not to add the name Bathsheba.

Is naturalness a good enough reason to make this kind of addition? The translators of the NASB evidently thought so. Besides adding the name Bathsheba, they made two other adjustments to this verse that appear to be based solely on naturalness.

Adjustment 5: The Word "and" Was Omitted
In Greek, this sentence starts out by saying, "*and* David fathered Solomon."[22] The NASB translators chose to omit this occurrence of the word *and*. But this is not the only place. They omitted it several other places in this passage as well.

In Greek, each generation of this lengthy genealogy is introduced with the word *and* (Gk *de*). The KJV and the ESV translated this pattern literally from Greek. Here is how the KJV translated Matthew 1:4-6a (emphasis added):

> *And* Aram begat Aminadab; *and* Aminadab begat Naasson; *and* Naasson begat Salmon; *And* Salmon begat Booz of Rachab; *and* Booz begat Obed of Ruth; *and* Obed begat Jesse; *And* Jesse begat David the king; *and* David . . .

This reflects good literary style in Greek. But in English, it sounds a bit tedious and repetitive. Apparently that is why the NASB translators decided to omit the word *and* twenty-six times in this genealogy. The NKJV omitted it twenty-four times, and the HCSB, thirty-three times. The KJV and ESV chose to translate all thirty-eight occurrences (table 5.4).

---

[20]The KJV translators came to the same conclusion when they added the words "that had been."
[21]Some versions, including the ESV and HCSB, did not add any of these four words.
[22]In Greek word order, the word *and* (Gk *de*) follows the name David rather than preceding it.

Table 5.4

Matthew 1:1-16—"and"		
	Included	Omitted
Greek	38 times	
KJV	38 times	—
ESV	38 times	—
NASB	12 times	26 times
NKJV	14 times	24 times
HCSB	5 times[a]	33 times

[a] In two of these five instances, the HCSB appropriately translated *de* as "then" instead of "and."

Does that mean that the KJV and ESV translated these verses faithfully, and the NASB, NKJV and HCSB were unfaithful? Certainly not! It was perfectly fine for the KJV and ESV to translate all thirty-eight occurrences. But the decision by the other three versions to omit many of them does not make them any less faithful or accurate. I do not believe the inspired text of this passage has been compromised. We have already seen that the true test of faithfulness and accuracy goes much deeper than a simple word count.

The meaning of this passage is the same in all five of these versions. The difference is that the ESV and KJV decided to translate that meaning in a form resembling Greek literary style, and the NASB, NKJV and HCSB decided to translate the same meaning in a form more closely reflecting English literary style.

This suggests an additional axiom. At least in this case, the NASB, NKJV and HCSB translators concluded that stylistic naturalness has priority over literally translating each word of the original. When the translators of the NASB, NKJV and HCSB left out these occurrences of the word *and*, they did so with full assurance that they were not violating the second part of the warning in Revelation 22, which warns against taking away from the words of Scripture.

Adjustment 6: A Greek Verb Was Replaced with an English Noun

Some readers may assume that literal versions of the New Testament match each Greek verb with an English verb and each Greek noun with an English noun. That is not necessarily true. In this verse, the translators of the NASB chose to replace a Greek verb with an English noun, set in a state-of-being clause. Consider this comparison.

Table 5.5

Greek wording	*David **fathered** Solomon*
NASB	*David was the father of Solomon*[a]

[a] The wording of this part of the verse in the ESV and NIV is identical to that of the NASB.

It is possible to match this Greek verb with an English verb, as the KJV did, translating it "begat." But the verb *begat* is outdated and is no longer natural in English. For that reason, the translators of the NASB, ESV and NIV determined (thirty-nine times in this passage) that in translating this Greek verb, a contemporary noun is preferable to a more literal yet archaic verb. Also, at least in this case, they determined that it is preferable to substitute a natural form in place of an unnatural form, even if it means changing it to a different part of speech (e.g., a noun in place of a verb).

If the translators of these versions had felt that it was important to reflect the verb form of the original, they could have updated the KJV verb *begat* to "fathered."[23] But that would not have been natural either, because "fathered" is not a commonly used verb in English. Also, there could be a problem of wrong connotation. The connotation of the verb *fathered* is a small step away from "sired" and could imply that David did not have a fatherly relationship of any real substance with Solomon, as though Solomon were nothing more than David's biological offspring. The NASB, ESV and NIV translators apparently decided that translating a verb for a verb in this case was not worth the degree of naturalness or correct connotation they would have had to sacrifice to do so.

Not Strictly Form-Based

So we find that the translators of the NASB made several significant adjustments in their translation of this seemingly simple, nine-word Greek phrase. They omitted three Greek words, added eight English words[24] and replaced

---

[23]The HCSB used the word *fathered* here.

[24]Gk: Δαυὶδ δὲ ἐγέννησεν τὸν Σολομῶνα ἐκ τῆς τοῦ Οὐρίου.

Lit: *David and fathered the Solomon by the (her) of-the of-Uriah.*

NASB: *David **was the** father **of** Solomon by **Bathsheba who had been the wife** of Uriah.*

(Words in bold were added by the translators.)

a verb with a noun. Yet the inspired meaning of the original remains intact!
Here is a summary of these adjustments (table 5.6).

Table 5.6

Matthew 1:6b			
	English Words Added	Greek Words Omitted	Verb Changed to Noun
NASB	8	3	yes
ESV	4	2	yes
NIV	8	4	yes
HCSB[a]	1	3	no
NKJV	5	3	no
KJV	5	2	no

[a]In this verse, the HCSB appears to be the most literal of these six versions, but
that is not always the case, since the degree of literalness in all these versions
varies a great deal from passage to passage and verse to verse.

We can see by this verse that the translators of these versions did not base
every translation decision on the ideal of trying to match the original words.
We can also see that when they set aside the original form, it was not always
because of English grammar. Several of their adjustments were intended to
clarify the meaning and make the translation more natural and readable in
English. In the next few chapters, as we begin examining more of the evidence, I believe it will become increasingly apparent that English versions
presumed to be literal are not as literal as presumed.

6

Divine Inspiration

Do Not Judge the "Logos" by Its Cover

◆ ◆ ◆

No prophecy of scripture ever comes about by the prophet's
own imagination, for no prophecy was ever borne
of human impulse; rather, men carried along
by the Holy Spirit spoke from God.

2 Peter 1:20-21 (net)

All Scripture is God-breathed
and is useful for teaching, rebuking, correcting
and training in righteousness.

2 Timothy 3:16 (niv)

No discussion about Bible translation would be complete without looking into the matter of divine inspiration. How does the doctrine of inspiration affect the practice of translation? Does a truly biblical doctrine of inspiration require all translators to embrace only certain translation ideals? We will explore these questions in a moment, but first we need to clarify what we mean by the term "inspiration."

A GROWING DEFINITION

Charles Ryrie gives an excellent explanation of the confusion that can arise from an inadequate definition of inspiration:

> Although those holding many theological viewpoints would be willing to say the Bible is inspired, one finds little uniformity as to what is meant by inspiration. Some focus it on the writers; others, on the writings; still others, on the readers. Some relate it to the general message of the Bible; others, to the thoughts; still others, to the words. Some include inerrancy; many don't. These differences call for precision in stating the biblical doctrine. Formerly all that was necessary to affirm one's belief in full inspiration was the statement, "I believe in the inspiration of the Bible." But when some did not extend inspiration to the words of the text, it became necessary to say, "I believe in the verbal inspiration of the Bible." To counter the teaching that not all parts of the Bible were inspired, one had to say, "I believe in the verbal, plenary inspiration of the Bible." Then because some did not want to ascribe total accuracy to the Bible, it was necessary to say, "I believe in the verbal, plenary, infallible, inerrant inspiration of the Bible." But then "infallible" and "inerrant" began to be limited to matters of faith only rather than also embracing all that the Bible records (including historical facts, genealogies, accounts of Creation, etc.), so it became necessary to add the concept of "unlimited inerrancy." Each addition to the basic statement arose because of an erroneous teaching.[1]

I fully embrace the verbal, plenary, wholly infallible and inerrant inspiration of the Bible as Ryrie has described it here. But even this expanded definition may not go far enough, as I will explain in a later chapter.

In the context of Bible translation, the discussion of inspiration usually turns to the matter of verbal inspiration, focusing on the words of the text. Are the actual words of Scripture inspired? Of course they are! Every detail of the original is "the product of the creative breath of God."[2] But what does that mean for translation? Does it mean every word in the original must be represented by a word (or combination of words) in our translations of Scripture?[3]

---

[1] C. C. Ryrie, *Basic Theology: A Popular Systematic Guide to Understanding Biblical Truth* (Chicago: Moody Press, 1999), p. 76.

[2] B. B. Warfield, *The Inspiration and Authority of the Bible* (Philadelphia: Presbyterian and Reformed, 1948), p. 133.

[3] Cf. Gordon D. Fee and Mark L. Strauss, *How to Choose a Translation for All Its Worth* (Grand Rapids: Zondervan, 2007), pp. 35-36.

It has been suggested that any translator who does not attempt to produce a word-for-word translation must not believe that the actual words of Scripture are inspired. Is that accusation fair? How can we know whether the translators of any particular version believe in verbal inspiration? What kind of questions should we ask to be assured they do? Let me suggest a few:

- Did the translators translate word for word?

- Did they omit some of the original words from their translation?

- Did they add words that do not represent words in the original?

- Did they replace single words with phrases?

- Did they translate concepts (or thoughts) in place of words?

- Did they replace biblical terms with present-day equivalent terms?

In this chapter, we will explore each of these questions. There is another important question, which we will examine separately in chapter 9:

- Did the translators inject interpretation into their translation of Scripture?

TRANSLATING WORD FOR WORD

We saw in previous chapters how difficult it can be to translate the Scriptures word for word into English. For example, the KJV, NASB and ESV together translated the Greek word *logos* ("word") more than fifty different ways.[4] There are many similar examples throughout Scripture. Let us look at a few from the Old Testament.

One Hebrew Word Translated Many Different Ways

The Hebrew word *tôb*, which is normally defined as "good," is translated in the KJV by all the terms listed in the following chart (table 6.1), plus four idiomatic renderings, for a total of forty-one renderings. Notice that the list of English renderings for this one Hebrew word includes nouns, verbs, adjectives and adverbs—also single words and multiple-word phrases.

---

[4]See chap. 4, tables 4.2 and 4.4.

Table 6.1

צוֹב (tôb), "good" in the KJV[a]			
beautiful	fine	graciously	pleasure
best	glad	joyful	precious
better	good	kindly	prosperity
bountiful	good deed	kindness	ready
cheerful	goodlier	liketh	sweet
at ease	goodliest	liketh best	wealth
fair	goodly	loving	welfare
fair word	goodness	merry	well
to favour	goods	pleasant	to be well
be in favour			
Plus 4 idiomatic renderings for a total of 41[b]			

[a] Robert Young, *Literal Translation of the Holy Bible* (1862), introduction.
[b] Ibid. Young does not list these "idiomatic renderings"; he simply states that they exist. This applies to tables 6.2 through 6.4 as well.

Here are a few more examples.

Table 6.2

נָתַן (nātan), "to give" in the KJV[a]			
add	direct	let out	restore
apply	distribute	lift up	send
appoint	fasten	make	send out
ascribe	frame	O that	set
assign	give	occupy	set forth
bestow	give forth	offer	shew
bring	give over	ordain	shoot forth
bring forth	give up	pay	shoot up
cast	grant	perform	strike
cause	hang	place	suffer
charge	hang up	pour	thrust
come	lay	print	trade
commit	lay to charge	put	turn
consider	lay up	put forth	utter
count	leave	recompense	would God
deliver	lend	render	yield
deliver up	let	requite	
Plus 17 idiomatic renderings for a total of 84			

[a] Robert Young, *Literal Translation of the Holy Bible.*

Table 6.3

עָשָׂה ('āśâh), "to do" in the KJV[a]			
accomplish	deck	grant	procure
advance	do	hold	provide
appoint	dress	keep	put
be at	execute	labour	require
bear	exercise	maintain	sacrifice
bestow	fashion	make ready	serve
bring forth	finish	make	set
bring to pass	fit	observe	shew
bruise	fulfil	offer	spend
be busy	furnish	pare	take
have charge	gather	perform	trim
commit	get	practice	work
deal	go about	prepare	yield
deal with	govern		
Plus 20 idiomatic renderings for a total of 74			

[a] Robert Young, *Literal Translation of the Holy Bible.*

Table 6.4

פָּנִים (pānîm), "face" in the KJV[a]			
afore	for	of	state
afore-time	forefront	off	straight
against	forepart	of old	through
anger	form	old time	till
at	former time	open	time past
because of	forward	over-against	times past
before	from	person	to
before-time	front	presence	toward
countenance	heaviness	prospect	unto
edge	it	was purposed	upon
face	as long as	by reason of	upside
favour	looks	right forth	with
fear of	mouth	sight	within
Plus 42 idiomatic renderings for a total of 94			

[a] Robert Young, *Literal Translation of the Holy Bible.*

I suppose we could generate a hundred pages of charts like these, if we took the time to do so, because this is a common feature of translation.[5] The reality is that no translator has ever been able to achieve word-for-word correspondence with any real degree of consistency.

In presenting these charts, it is not my aim to single out the KJV. I used these examples from the KJV because Robert Young (translator of *Young's Literal Translation*) kindly compiled them into easy-to-use lists more than one hundred years ago. If we were to do a similar analysis of the ESV and NASB translations, we would find essentially the same results.

The simple, clear-cut evidence in these charts suggests two more axioms that the translators of literal versions (like the KJV) have embraced:

- Translating the correct thought in each context often takes priority over the ideal of giving a transparent, word-for-word rendering.

- It is standard practice to translate some Hebrew or Greek words dozens of different ways in English, sometimes changing them to a noun, a verb, an adjective, an adverb or a multiple-word phrase.

Many Different Words Translated the Same

Just as one Hebrew or Greek word can represent many English words, so one English word can represent many Hebrew or Greek words. For example, the English word *destroy* in the KJV does not represent just one word in the original. Any time you see the word *destroy* in the King James Old Testament, it represents one of at least forty different Hebrew words (table 6.5).

Table 6.5

Hebrew Words Translated "Destroy" in the KJV [a]				
אָבַד	הוּם	חָרַם	מַשְׁחִית	צָדָה
אָבַד	הָמַם	יָנָה	נָסַח	צָמַת
אַל תַּשְׁחֵת	הָרַג	כָּלָה	נָקַף	קוּר
אָשַׁם	הָרַס	כָּרַת	נָשַׁם	שָׁבַר
נָרַר	חָבַל	כָּתַת	נָתַץ	שָׁדַד
דְּכָא	חֶבֶל	מָגַר	נָתַשׁ	שׁוֹא
דְּמָה	חָרַב	מוּל	סָפָה	שָׁחַת
דְּמָה	חָרַב	מָחָה	סָתַר	שָׁמֵם

[a] Compiled from *The Brown-Driver-Briggs Hebrew and English Lexicon* (Peabody, MA: Hendrickson, 1996).

---

[5] There are several more lists like these in the introduction to *Young's Literal Translation*.

Nothing in our English versions tells us which of these Hebrew words occurs in any given context. The only way to know for sure is to look it up.

There are many other individual words in our English versions that represent multiple Hebrew words. For example, there are twenty-two Hebrew words that the KJV translated "to be afraid," and there are forty Hebrew words translated "to set."

In table 6.6, each Old Testament word or phrase is listed along with the number of different Hebrew words it represents in the KJV.

Table 6.6

English Term (in the KJV) + Number of Different Hebrew Words[a]			
to abhor 12	abide 13	abundance 11	affliction 12
to be afraid 22	after 13	against 13	among 11
to be angry 10	another 11	to appoint 24	appointed 10
army 10	at 13	to bear 13	beauty 15
before 22	beside 14	to bind 15	body 12
border 13	bough 13	branch 20	to break 33
bright 10	to bring 39	to bring forth 21	broken 12
to be broken 16	to burn 19	burning 12	but 15
by 14	captain 16	captivity 10	to carry away 10
to carry 12	to cast 19	to cast down 19	to cast out 15
to catch 12	to cease 21	chain 10	chamber 10
change 16	to be changed 10	chief 10	to cleave 15
coast 10	to come 32	commandment 12	companion 10
company 22	to consider 18	to consume 21	consumed 10
to continue 11	corner 10	country 10	to cover 21
covering 13	to cry 17	to cut down 10	be cut down 13
to cut off 18	to be cut off 14	dark 11	darkness 10
to declare 11	decree 11	to be defiled 10	to deliver 26
to depart 18	desire 13	to desire 13	desolate 16
to be desolate 11	desolation 12	to despise 10	destroyer 8
to be destroyed 17	destruction 35	to divide 19	to draw out 10
dung 10	to dwell 14	dwelling 11	east 10
end 26	to establish 13	to be exalted 11	excellent 10
to fail 30	to faint 18	to fall 14	fear 16
to fear 10	flood 10	for 21	foundation 11
from 17	fruit 12	garment 14	to gather 23
to gather together 16	to be gathered 10	gathered together 14	to get 16
gift 12	to give 15	glorious 12	glory 10
to go 22	goodly 15	governor 12	great 24

[a] Robert Young, *Literal Translation of the Holy Bible* (1862), introduction.

English Term (in the KJV) + Number of Different Hebrew Words[a]			
grief 10	to be grieved 17	grievous 10	to grow 13
habitation 17	to harden 10	haste 11	to make haste 10
height 11	to hide 14	to hide self 12	high 18
to hold 12	hurt 11	idol 11	if 10
in 13	to increase 17	iniquity 11	to be joined 10
judgment 10	to keep 11	to kindle 15	knowledge 12
labour 10	laid down 10	to lay 24	to lead 12
to leave 15	to be left 11	to lift up 15	light 13
to long 10	to look 16	to be made 11	majesty 10
to make 23	man 12	to mark 10	measure 13
meat 14	to meet 10	midst 10	might 12
mighty 26	to mourn 12	to move 15	to be moved 13
much 10	multitude 14	net 10	not 14
now 13	of 10	to offer 22	offering 10
old 13	only 11	to oppress 10	to ordain 12
over 10	to overthrow 11	palace 10	part 14
people 10	to perceive 10	to perish 13	pit 12
place 13	pleasant 17	pleasure 10	poor 10
portion 13	to pour out 12	power 17	to prepare 14
to prevail 15	pride 10	prince 11	proud 16
to put 28	to regard 17	rejoice 19	to remain 16
remnant 11	to remove 20	to be removed 11	to repair 10
to rest 17	reward 16	riches 10	right 16
river 11	ruler 13	to run 14	scatter 12
to be scattered 10	secret 12	to set 40	to be set 13
to set up 18	to shake 15	to shew 19	to shine 11
to shut 11	side 13	to be slain 14	slaughter 12
to slay 15	to smite 12	sorrow 28	to speak 22
speech 10	spoil 10	to spoil 16	to spread 15
to stay 14	to stop 10	strength 33	to strengthen 12
strong 26	substance 14	to take 34	to take away 24
taken away 10	to tarry 16	to teach 10	to tell 12
terror 10	that 16	these 16	think 12
this 20	thought 11	through 11	thus 10
to 12	tremble 13	trouble 14	to trouble 12
to be troubled 14	truth 11	to turn 15	to turn aside 10
to be turned 10	understanding 14	to utter 15	to vex 16
to wait 10	wall 13	waste 10	to waste 10
when 12	where 13	which 11	wisdom 12
with 18	within 12	without 12	word 10
work 15	wrath 10	yet 10	youth 11

The evidence in the preceding charts (tables 6.5 and 6.6) points to yet another translation axiom: It is often necessary to translate many different Hebrew words exactly the same way in English.

Omitting Words[6]

There are places in every English version where the translators chose to omit a particular Hebrew or Greek word rather than to reflect it literally in their translation. An example of this is the Hebrew word *nepeš*, which is most often translated "soul."[7] The Hebrew text of Job 36:14 includes this word, but most English versions left it out, including many of those that are considered word-for-word translations. Compare the Hebrew wording of this verse with the way the following versions translated it.

Table 6.7

Job 36:14	
Hebrew wording	*Their **soul** is dying in youth*
YLT	*Their **soul** dieth in youth*
ESV	*They die in youth*
NASB	*They die in youth*
KJV	*They die in youth*
HCSB	*They die in their youth*

None of these versions left out any of the meaning even though four of them did not literally translate the Hebrew word *nepeš*. In this context, *nepeš* is functioning as a figure of speech called synecdoche, in which a part of something is used to represent the whole or the whole is used to represent a part. The translators of these versions recognized that the phrase "their soul" represents the whole person ("they"). This is clearly an example of translating thought for thought rather than word for word.

In the New Testament, the Greek word for "soul" *(psychē)* can also work this way. Look at the HCSB and KJV translations of 2 Corinthians 12:15 in

---

[6]See Wayne Grudem, "Are Only *Some* Words of Scripture Breathed Out by God? Why Plenary Inspiration Favors 'Essentially Literal' Bible Translation," in C. John Collins, Wayne Grudem, Vern Sheridan Poythress, Leland Ryken and Bruce Winter, *Translating Truth: The Case for Essentially Literal Bible Translation* (Wheaton, IL: Crossway, 2005), pp. 30-45.
[7]Ibid., pp. 37-38, under the heading "The Lost Soul."

table 6.8. This time the NASB and ESV chose to include the word *soul*, even
though they left it out in other similar verses.

Table 6.8

2 Corinthians 12:15[a]	
Greek wording	*I will very gladly . . . be spent for your **souls***
ESV	*I will most gladly . . . be spent for your **souls***
NASB	*I will most gladly . . . be spent for your **souls***
HCSB	*I will most gladly . . . be spent for you*
KJV	*I will very gladly . . . be spent for you*

[a] This is not based on a textual difference. The reading of this part of the verse in
the Textus Receptus is identical to that of the Critical Text.

Another example is in John 10:24 (see table 6.9). This time none of these
versions literally translated the word *soul* (Gk *psychē*). They translated the
figurative thoughts rather than the literal words.

Table 6.9

John 10:24	
Greek wording	*How long do you hold our **souls** [in suspense]?*[a]
ESV	*How long will you keep us in suspense?*
NASB	*How long will You keep us in suspense?*
HCSB	*How long are You going to keep us in suspense?*
KJV	*How long dost thou make us to doubt?*

[a] The word *soul* is literally reflected in this verse in WYCLIFFE and YLT.

Here are two more Old Testament examples.

Table 6.10

Leviticus 2:1	
Hebrew wording	*When any **soul** brings a grain offering*[a]
ESV	*When anyone brings a grain offering*
NASB	*when anyone presents a grain offering*
HCSB	*When anyone brings a grain offering*
KJV	*when any will offer a meat offering*

[a] The word *soul* is literally reflected in this verse in TYNDALE.

Table 6.11

Genesis 27:25	
Hebrew wording	*that my* **soul** *may bless you*[a]
KJV	*that my* **soul** *may bless thee*
ESV	*that I may . . . bless you*
HCSB	*that I can bless you*
NASB	*that I may bless you*

[a] The word *soul* is also explicated in this verse in the NKJV, WYCLIFFE and TYNDALE.

Why did the ESV, HCSB and NASB choose not to translate the word *soul* literally in this verse?[8] Did English grammar require that they leave it out?[9] No. The phrase "that my soul may bless you" fits well within the bounds of English grammar rules. In fact, it almost sounds poetic—perhaps adding a dimension of richness to the verse. Did the translators omit this word to avoid communicating wrong or unclear meaning? I doubt it. A literal translation of the phrase "that my soul may bless you" seems to make the intended meaning clear.[10]

The only apparent reason for omitting the word *soul* in this and other verses is for the sake of naturalness: We do not say it that way in contemporary English. If the translators of the ESV, HCSB and NASB had literally translated Genesis 27:25 as "that my soul may bless you," it would have given a more transparent view of the original words. However, the translators of these versions decided that it is acceptable to set aside the ideal of transparency to the original text (even when they do not have to) solely for the sake of naturalness.

"God" Omitted?

Sometimes, it appears that even "God" has been left out of some English translations. The most common word for "God" in the Hebrew Old Testament is *ĕlōhîm*. There are a number of places where *ĕlōhîm* was explicitly translated "God" in some versions but not in others. These differences do

---

[8] There are many more places in Scripture where some or all of these versions did not literally reflect the word *soul*. Here are a few: 1 Sam 1:10; 2 Kings 4:27; Job 16:4; Ps 141:8; Eccles 7:28; Is 26:9; 32:6; 44:20; 51:23; 53:10, 12; 55:3; 56:11; Jer 4:31; 6:8; 14:19; 18:20; 38:17, 20; 44:14; Ezek 16:5; 23:17, 18, 22, 28; Jon 2:7; Mic 7:1; Acts 2:43; 2 Cor 1:23; Heb 12:3; Jas 1:21; 1 Pet 1:22; 2:11; Rev 18:14.
[9] See the Adjustment Flowchart (figure 5.1).
[10] The ESV literally translated *nepeš* as "soul" in the similar phrase "that your soul may bless me" in Gen 27:19.

not represent variations in the Hebrew manuscripts; they are a matter of interpretation on the part of the translators.[11]

In Genesis 30:8, the HCSB translated *ĕlōhîm* as "God," but most other versions chose not to (table 6.12).

Table 6.12

Genesis 30:8	
Hebrew wording	*twistings of ĕlōhîm*[a]
HCSB	*wrestlings with **God***
KJV	*great wrestlings*
NASB	*mighty wrestlings*
ESV	*mighty wrestlings*

[a] The NASB footnote for this verse says "Lit *wrestlings of God*."

In Genesis 23:6, the ESV and HCSB included "God," but the NASB and KJV did not (table 6.13).

Table 6.13

Genesis 23:6	
Hebrew wording	*prince of ĕlōhîm*
ESV	*prince of **God***
HCSB	***God's** chosen one*
NASB	*mighty prince*
KJV	*mighty prince*

In 1 Samuel 14:15, the NIV and GW included the word *God*, but the ESV, NASB and KJV left it out (table 6.14).

Table 6.14

1 Samuel 14:15	
Hebrew wording	*trembling (or "panic") of ĕlōhîm*
NIV	*panic sent by **God***
GW	*panic sent from **God***
ESV	*very great panic*
NASB	*great trembling*
KJV	*very great trembling*

[11] The question in each case is whether the translators interpreted *ĕlōhîm* to be literal or figurative. Where they interpreted it to be literal, they translated it "God"; where they interpreted it as figurative, they translated it some other way: "great" or "mighty." See also Jonah 3:3.

In Genesis 35:5, the NASB is one of very few English versions that left out the word *God*. Most other versions included it—not only versions that are generally considered literal but also dynamic equivalence versions like the NLT and CEV (table 6.15).[12]

Table 6.15

Genesis 35:5	
Hebrew wording	*terror of ĕlōhîm*
ESV	*terror from* **God**
KJV	*terror of* **God**
NIV	*terror of* **God**
NLT	*terror from* **God**
NASB	*great terror*
MESSAGE	*paralyzing fear*

Apart from the NASB, the only widely used English Bible I could find that left "God" out of this verse is the MESSAGE. In this case, the NASB and the MESSAGE stand alone together. They form an unlikely twosome indeed, since the NASB describes itself as the "Most Literal"[13] and the MESSAGE is arguably the least literal among current, popular English Bibles.

More Omissions in the "Most Literal" Versions

Below are a few more places where the NASB omitted some of the original words.[14] That is not to say that the NASB omits more words than other versions; on the contrary, it probably omits fewer than most. But any omission of verbally inspired words from the "most literal"[15] version is worth noting (tables 6.16 through 6.19).[16]

Table 6.16

Ezekiel 1:7	
Hebrew wording	**the soles of** *their feet*
NKJV	**the soles of** *their feet*
ESV	**the soles of** *their feet*
HCSB	**the soles of** *their feet*
NASB	— *their feet*

[12]English versions that translated *ĕlōhîm* as "God" in this verse include AMP, ASV, CEV, ESV, GW, KJV, NCV, NET, NIV, NKJV, NLT, NRSV, HCSB, VOICE, YLT, plus others.
[13]Updated NASB (1995), title page.
[14]These particular words are also omitted in the NIV, NLT, CEV and other nonliteral versions.
[15]Updated NASB (1995), title page.
[16]The Hebrew wording in these four examples is from the NASB footnotes for these verses.

Table 6.17

Jeremiah 38:4		
Hebrew wording	*the hands of*	*all the people*
NKJV	*the hands of*	*all the people*
ESV	*the hands of*	*all the people*
NASB[a]	—	*all the people*[b]

[a] Also omitted in the HCSB.
[b] See Grudem, "Are Only *Some* Words of Scripture Breathed Out by God?" pp. 35-37, under the heading "The Missing Hands."

Table 6.18

Ezekiel 1:13		
Hebrew wording	like *the appearance of* torches	
NKJV	like *the appearance of* torches	
ESV	like *the appearance of* torches	
NASB	like — torches	

Table 6.19

Zephaniah 3:10		
Hebrew wording	*the daughter of* My dispersed ones	
NJKV	*the daughter of* My dispersed ones	
ESV	*the daughter of* My dispersed ones	
NASB	— My dispersed ones[a]	

[a] Also HCSB.

Omissions like these can be found in every literal version. Tables 6.20 and 6.21 illustrate two more places where the ESV chose to omit some of the original words even though other versions included them.

Table 6.20

Genesis 34:26		
Hebrew wording	*Shechem . . . they killed with **the edge of** the sword*[a]	
NASB	*They killed . . . Shechem with **the edge of** the sword*	
NKJV	*They killed . . . Shechem with **the edge of** the sword*	
ESV	*They killed . . . Shechem with — the sword*[b]	

[a] In this case, the omitted part ("the edge of") represents just one word in Hebrew.
[b] Also omitted in the HCSB.

Table 6.21

Micah 2:7	
Hebrew wording	*Has the **spirit** of the Lord grown short?* [a]
NASB	*Is the **Spirit** of the Lord impatient?*
HCSB	*Is the **Spirit** of the Lord impatient?*
NLT	*Will the Lord's **Spirit** have patience?* [b]
ESV	*Has — the Lord grown impatient?* [c]

[a] The Hebrew wording in this example is from the ESV footnote for this verse.
[b] The word *Spirit* is also literally reflected in this verse in *The Voice Bible* (VOICE).
[c] See Grudem, "Are Only *Some* Words of Scripture Breathed Out by God?" pp. 38-39, under the heading "The Lost Spirit." In order to make that argument more complete and more objective, it would perhaps be good to include this example where the NLT literally reflected the Hebrew word for "Spirit" and the ESV chose not to.

Omitted for the Sake of Appropriateness

Translators have sometimes omitted certain Greek or Hebrew words for the sake of appropriateness. An example is the Greek word *aphedrōn*, which means "latrine" or "toilet." It occurs only twice in the New Testament (Mt 15:17; Mk 7:19). Johannes Louw and Eugene Nida make the following comment about this word: "In some languages . . . a reference to a toilet may seem inappropriate for the Scriptures."[17]

The translators of several literal English versions, including the NASB, NKJV and ESV, apparently agreed with Louw and Nida, because they omitted the phrase *eis aphedrōna* ("into a latrine") from their translations.[18] Compare the Greek wording (set in English word order) with the way the versions in table 6.22 translated this phrase.

Table 6.22

Matthew 15:17 and Mark 7:19	
Greek wording	*[it] is eliminated **into a latrine**.* [a]
NASB	*[it] is eliminated.*
NKJV	*[it] is eliminated.*
HCSB	*[it] is eliminated.*
ESV	*[it] is expelled.*

[a] Some English versions that included this phrase translated it as follows: "into the drain" (YLT); "into the sewer" (NET, NRSV, NLT); "into a toilet" (GW); "into the draught" (KJV, ASV, TYNDALE); "into the going away" (WYCLIFFE).

---

[17] Johannes P. Louw and Eugene A. Nida, eds., *Greek-English Lexicon of the New Testament based on Semantic Domains* (New York: United Bible Societies, 1988), item 7.72.
[18] Most idiomatic versions also omitted this phrase.

Did the translators of these versions think these particular words were not inspired?[19] Of course not. Why then did they leave some of God's inspired words out of their translations? The answer is clear; all of these omissions (plus thousands of others we have not mentioned) are based on one or more of the four criteria for adjustment presented in chapter 5.[20] Interestingly, the highly idiomatic New Living Translation (NLT 2004) translated this phrase "into the sewer." This is another case where the NLT is more literal than word-for-word translations such as the ESV, NASB, NKJV and others.[21]

The translators of every literal version have adopted the ideal of seeking to give a transparent rendering of each word in the original, but word-for-word transparency is not their only ideal. In fact, transparency often is bumped to the end of the line behind a string of other more important ideals, such as meaning, grammar, clarity, naturalness and appropriateness.[22] These higher ideals provide the rationale that allowed many translators to omit words or phrases like "soul" and "into a latrine." So while every word of Scripture has been breathed out by God, that does not mean they are all directly reflected in any of our English versions.

The preceding examples suggest another translation axiom. The translators of these versions concluded, at least in these cases, that naturalness and appropriateness have priority over the ideal of seeking to give a transparent, word-for-word view into the original text. In addition, these translators apparently concluded that in some contexts, naturalness and appropriateness[23] are justifiable reasons for omitting certain Hebrew and Greek words or phrases and not reflecting them in their translations.

ADDING WORDS[24]

Just as every version has omitted some of the original words, so every version has added words to their translations that do not represent any

---

[19]Cf. Grudem, "Are Only *Some* Words of Scripture Breathed Out by God?"

[20]The criteria for adjustment are grammar, meaning, clarity and naturalness. See chap. 5, figure 5.1.

[21]*God's Word* translation (GW) also opted for a more literal rendering than the ESV, NASB, HCSB and NKJV, translating this phrase "into a toilet."

[22]In the adjustment flowchart (chap. 5, figure 5.1), "appropriateness" is part of the correct meaning; it is a feature of the dynamics (chap. 2, "The Dynamics of Meaning").

[23]"Appropriateness" is also the reason that several versions, including the NASB and ESV, replaced the phrase "one who urinates against the wall" with the abbreviated phrase "one male" (1 Sam 25:22, 34; 1 Kings 14:10; 16:11).

[24]See Grudem, "Are Only *Some* Words of Scripture Breathed Out by God?" pp. 45-48.

actual words in the original. Let us look again at Matthew 1:6.[25] In this verse, the ESV gives a semi-transparent view into the original wording, translating it "David was the father of Solomon by the wife of Uriah." But the NASB added the four-word phrase "Bathsheba who had been" (table 6.23).

Table 6.23

Matthew 1:6				
ESV	*the father of Solomon by*	—		*the wife of Uriah*
NASB	*the father of Solomon by*	**Bathsheba who had been**		*the wife of Uriah*

In Acts 9:36 the NASB translators added the explanatory phrase "in Greek." Many other versions chose not to add this phrase (table 6.24).

Table 6.24

Acts 9:36				
HCSB	*Tabitha, which is translated*	—		*Dorcas*
NET	*Tabitha (which in translation*	—		*means Dorcas)*
NASB	*Tabitha (which translated*	**in Greek**		*is called Dorcas)*

When the NASB translators added the words "in Greek" to this verse, they stepped outside of their ideal range and chose a rendering on the idiomatic side of the spectrum (figure 6.1). In this case, the NASB sided with idiomatic versions such as the NLT, NIV and TEV.

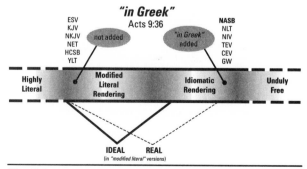

Fig. 6.1

Below are a few more places where the NASB added words that are not in the original, while some other versions considered it unnecessary.

Table 6.25

Matthew 1:24			
ESV	*he took*	—	*his wife*
NASB	*he took*	**Mary as**	*his wife*

Table 6.26

Matthew 2:22			
NIV	*having been warned*	—	*in a dream*
HCSB	*being warned*	—	*in a dream*
NASB	*being warned*	**by God**	*in a dream*

Table 6.27

Matthew 6:4			
HCSB	*your Father who sees*	—	*in secret*
NKJV	*your Father who sees*	—	*in secret*
VOICE	*your Father, who sees*	—	*in secret*
NASB	*your Father who sees*	**what is done**	*in secret*

Table 6.28

Acts 1:2			
HCSB	*until the day He was taken up,*	—	*after He*
NKJV	*until the day in which he was taken up,*	—	*after he*
NASB	*until the day when he was taken up*	**to heaven**	*after he*

Table 6.29

Acts 28:8			
NLT	*ill with*	—	*fever and dysentery*
NIV	*suffering from*	—	*fever and dysentery*
HCSB	*suffering from*	—	*fever and dysentery*
NASB	*afflicted with*	**recurrent**	*fever and dysentery*

In Romans 12:6 the NASB and ESV each added an extra phrase to clarify the overarching meaning of the passage (table 6.30).

Table 6.30

Romans 12:6			
KJV	*gifts differing according to the grace that is given to us,*	—	*whether prophecy*[a]
NASB	*gifts that differ according to the grace that is given to us,*	**each of us is to exercise them accordingly:**	*if prophecy*
ESV	*gifts that differ according to the grace that is given to us,*	**let us use them:**	*if prophecy*

[a] Even though the KJV did not add words at this particular place, it did add words and phrases in other parts of the passage.

Both of these added phrases are acceptable, but neither represents any actual words from the original. Here, the translators set aside their ideal of word-for-word translation in order to reflect important, additional meaning they felt was implied above the word level.[26]

As a general rule, meaning-based versions such as the NIV add words more frequently than literal versions do. However, in the following two examples, the NIV opted for an essentially literal rendering while the NASB and ESV added extra words which do not represent any actual words from the original.

Table 6.31

Matthew 10:25			
NIV	*how much more*	—	*the members of his household*[a]
NASB	*how much more*	**will they malign**	*the members of his household*
ESV	*how much more*	**will they malign**	*the members of his household*

[a] Also HCSB.

Table 6.32

1 Corinthians 14:22			
NIV	*prophecy, however, is*	—	*not for unbelievers*[a]
NASB	*but prophecy is for*	**a sign**	*not to unbelievers*
ESV	*while prophecy is*	**a sign**	*not for unbelievers*

[a] Also HCSB and NKJV.

[26] See chap. 5, "Explicit and Implicit Information."

The NASB and ESV translators determined, at least in these cases, that it is acceptable to add optional, explanatory words and phrases to fill out the meaning in this way.

REPLACING A WORD WITH A PHRASE

If we compare any idiomatic (or dynamic equivalence) version with the original text, it quickly becomes obvious that these versions often replace a single word in the original with a phrase. Literal versions, however, prefer to translate single words with single words. But in practice, literal versions replace words with phrases too; they just do not do that as often as idiomatic versions do. Table 6.33 shows several examples where a single Greek word was translated by a phrase in English. Most of these examples are from literal versions.

Table 6.33

Greek Word	English Phrases
deigmatisai (Mt 1:19)	"to make [her] a public example" (KJV, NKJV) "to put [her] to shame" (ESV)
grēgoreite (Mt 24:42)	"be on the alert." (NASB) "stay awake" (ESV)
mogilalon (Mk 7:32)	"had an impediment in his speech" (KJV) "had a speech impediment" (ESV) "spoke with difficulty" (NASB)
lepta (Mk 12:42)	"small copper coins" (NASB, ESV) "very small copper coins" (NIV)
prosabbaton (Mk 15:42)	"the day before the Sabbath" (NASB, ESV, KJV, NKJV)
antiparēlthen (Lk 10:31)	"he passed by on the other side" (KJV, NASB, ESV, NKJV)
ōrthrizen (Lk 21:38)	"came early in the morning" (KJV) "would get up early in the morning to come" (NASB)
cheiragōgous (Acts 13:11)	"those who would lead him by the hand" (NASB) "people to lead him by the hand" (ESV) "someone to lead him by the hand" (NKJV)
logos (Acts 15:27)	"word of mouth" (NASB, ESV, NKJV, HCSB, NET, NIV)
porphyropōlis (Acts 16:14)	"a seller of purple" (KJV, NKJV, YLT) "a seller of purple fabrics" (NASB) "a seller of purple goods" (ESV) "a dealer in purple cloth" (NET, HCSB)
hierosylous (Acts 19:37)	"robbers of churches" (KJV) "robbers of temples" (NKJV, NASB)

Greek Word	English Phrases
ethēriomachēsa (1 Cor 15:32)	"I fought with wild beasts" (NASB, NET) "I fought with beasts" (ESV) "I fought wild animals" (HCSB)
andrizesthe (1 Cor 16:13)	"quit you like men" (KJV) "act like men" (NASB, ESV) "be brave" (NKJV, HCSB)
anepaischynton (2 Tim 2:15)	"who does not need to be ashamed" (NASB, NKJV, NIV, NET) "who has no need to be ashamed" (ESV)
aphilagathoi (2 Tim 3:3)	"haters of good" (NASB) "not loving good" (ESV) "despisers of those that are good" (KJV) "without love for what is good" (HCSB)
theopneustos [a] (2 Tim 3:16)	"given by inspiration of God" (KJV) "inspired by God" (NASB, NET, HCSB) "breathed out by God" (ESV)
homoiopathēs (Jas 5:17)	"subject to like passions" (KJV) "with a nature like ours" (NASB, ESV, NKJV, HCSB)
allotriepiskopos (1 Pet 4:15)	"a busybody in other men's matters" (KJV) "a busybody in other people's matters" (NKJV)
aischrokerdōs (1 Pet 5:2)	"for filthy lucre" (KJV) "for dishonest gain" (NKJV) "for sordid gain" (NASB) "for shameful gain" (ESV) "for shameful profit" (NET)

[a] In this case, the NIV has perhaps come closer than any other popular English version in producing a literal, formal equivalent of the Greek word *theopneustos* with its hyphenated, single-word rendering "God-breathed." The NASB footnote for this verse says "Lit *God-breathed.*"

These are only a few of the many places in Scripture where most English versions used a phrase to translate a single word from the original. In some of these cases, the translators had no choice, because no equivalent word exists in English.

For example, in Mark 15:42, the Greek word *prosabbaton* (table 6.33) means "the day before the sabbath." There is not much a translator could do other than translating this word as a phrase. However, Robert Young, in his *Literal Translation of the Bible*, invented a new term: "fore-sabbath." It is true that this single, hyphenated word gives a more transparent view into the Greek text than the phrase "the day before the sabbath." But it does not communicate the meaning as clearly, and it is not as natural. In translating this Greek word, the translators of virtually all other English versions concluded that a clear and natural phrase is preferable to a single word that is unclear and unnatural.

Another interesting example is the Greek word *porphyropōlis* (table 6.33) in

Acts 16:14. When John Wycliffe translated this verse in the fourteenth century, he coined the word *purpless* to describe Lydia's occupation, rather than using a phrase like "female seller of purple [cloth]." No other English version perpetuated this obscure, manufactured word. In this case, the translators of every major version determined that a single word in the original is sometimes best translated by a phrase in English. The translators of all these versions exchanged this word for a phrase because there was no reasonable alternative.

In some cases, however, translators have exchanged a word for a phrase even though there *was* a single-word alternative. For example, in 1 Peter 4:15, the Greek word *allotriepiskopos* (table 6.33) means "meddler." Several English versions translated it as such. However, the KJV and NKJV replaced this word with the phrase "a busybody in other men's/people's matters." Also, in Matthew 1:19, the Greek word *deigmatisai* (table 6.33) means "disgrace." The NASB translated it that way, but several other versions replaced this single word with a phrase even though they did not have to. The KJV and NKJV translated it "make [her] a public example"; the ESV translated it "put [her] to shame."

There are many other places in Scripture where translators have chosen to use a phrase even though a single-word rendering would have been a viable option. Here are a few more examples from the KJV (table 6.34).

Table 6.34

Greek Word	English Word	KJV Rendering as a Phrase
allophylō (Acts 10:28)	"foreigner"[a]	"one of another nation"
anamimnēskō (Heb 10:32)	"remember"[b] or "recall"[c]	"call to remembrance"
desmophylax (Acts 16:27, 36)	"jailer"[d]	"keeper of the prison"
hyperentynchanō (Rom 8:26)	"intercedes"[e]	"maketh intercession"

[a] NASB, HCSB.
[b] NASB, HCSB, NET, NIV, TEV.
[c] ESV, NKJV, NRSV.
[d] YLT, ESV, NASB, NRSV, HCSB, NET, NLT, TEV, NIV, VOICE.
[e] ESV, NASB, HCSB, NRSV, NET, NIV.

These examples show that the translators of every English version determined that it is acceptable to replace a single word with a phrase in many contexts—even when it is not absolutely necessary to do so.

TRANSLATING CONCEPTS

Some translation theorists claim that certain Bible versions translate concepts or thoughts, while other versions translate words. What does it mean to translate a concept? And what does it mean to translate a word?

Words and concepts do not exist in isolation from one another; instead, they are mutually dependent. Every word represents at least one concept, and every concept is communicated by part of a word, a complete word or a combination of words. It is impossible to translate a word without translating a concept at the same time. And in order to translate any word correctly, the translator needs to determine its underlying concept(s) in each context in which it occurs. Let us look at an illustration of this principle from Scripture. The Hebrew word *bārak* occurs more than three hundred times in the Old Testament. In the vast majority of occurrences, every English version translated it "bless." Here are some examples:

- "God blessed them, saying, 'Be fruitful and multiply'" (Gen 1:22 ESV)
- "I will bless you, And make your name great" (Gen 12:2 NASB)
- "and the children of Israel blessed God" (Josh 22:33 KJV)
- "Bless God in the congregations" (Ps 68:26 NASB)

In some cases, however, this same word is translated "curse" instead of "bless." Consider the five places that the word *bārak* occurs in the book of Job:

- "Perhaps my children have . . . cursed God in their hearts" (Job 1:5 NKJV)
- "he will curse you to your face" (Job 1:11; 2:5 ESV)
- "Blessed be the name of the LORD" (Job 1:21 NASB)
- "Curse God and die" (Job 2:9 NASB)

When Job's world fell apart, his wife told him to "bless God and die." Job knew that what she really meant was "curse God and die." The translators of our English versions knew that too. That is why they translated it that way instead of translating what she actually said. Every major English version translated the common Hebrew word for "bless" as "curse" four out of the five times it occurs in the book of Job.[27] The translators looked beyond the word

---

[27]In 1 Kings 21:10, 13, the KJV and NKJV translated *bārak* as "blaspheme." Most other versions translated it "curse" in these verses.

itself and translated the concept or thought behind the word in each context.

When the ancient Hebrews read the Scriptures aloud, the word *bārak* and its various forms were pronounced the same no matter what the context was. But the hearers knew that in some cases, the underlying concept or thought intended by the author was opposite the common meaning of the word. They knew that the common Hebrew word for "bless" was sometimes a euphemism for "curse."

If, in every case, the translators of our English versions had given priority to translating the precise word rather than translating its underlying concept, they would have corrupted the inspired meaning of God's Word in some contexts.

OTHER GRAMMATICAL CHANGES

It would be impossible to mention every kind of change that the translators of our English versions have made, but I will include examples of just two more grammatical areas: rhetorical questions (changed to statements) and substituting present-day equivalents. These examples further demonstrate that literal versions in English may not be as literal as some Christians believe them to be.

Rhetorical Questions Changed to Statements

In Genesis 16:13, the ESV replaced the original question with a statement; several other versions,[28] including the NLT, decided to keep the original question. This is one more instance where the NLT is more literal than the ESV.

Table 6.35

Genesis 16:13		
Hebrew wording	*Have I really seen him here who sees me?*[a]	(QUESTION)
NLT	*Have I truly seen the One who sees me?*	(QUESTION)
ESV	*Truly here I have seen him who looks after me.*	(STATEMENT)

[a] From the ESV footnote for this verse.

In 2 Samuel 23:19, the NIV and NKJV translated the rhetorical question literally. But the translators of the NASB and ESV apparently felt that this

---

[28] AMP, ASV, HCSB, KJV, NASB, NCV, NKJV, NLT, NRSV, TEV, YLT and others.

verse would be clearer and more natural if they eliminated the original question and replaced it with a statement (table 6.36).

Table 6.36

2 Samuel 23:19		
Hebrew wording	*Was he the most renowned?* [a]	QUESTION
NIV	*Was he not held in greater honor?*	QUESTION
NKJV	*Was he not the most honored?*	QUESTION
NASB	*He was most honored*	STATEMENT
ESV	*He was the most renowned*	STATEMENT

[a] This Hebrew translation is from the ESV footnote for this verse.

Substituting Present-Day Equivalents [29]

Much of the terminology in Scripture is unique to Bible times and Bible lands. Sometimes translators have transliterated the form of these terms, and sometimes they replaced them with modern-day terms.

For example, in table 6.37 below, the NIV and HCSB aimed for formal equivalence—transliterating the original word *Sanhedrin*. But the NASB and ESV followed the principle of dynamic equivalence, replacing the original word with their own contemporary terms.

Table 6.37

		Transliteration *(formal equivalent)*		Contemporary Term *(dynamic equivalent)*	
	Greek[a]	NIV[b]	HCSB	NASB	ESV
Mt 5:22	*Sanhedrin*	*Sanhedrin*[c]	*Sanhedrin*	Supreme Court	Council
Jn 11:47	*Sanhedrin*	Sanhedrin	Sanhedrin	council	council

[a] The Greek pronunciation is *sunedrion* (συνέδριον).
[b] The word *Sanhedrin* occurs twenty-two times in the New Testament. The NIV used a formal equivalent transliteration in eighteen of those twenty-two occurrences (Mt 26:59; Mk 14:55; 15:1; Jn 11:47; Acts 4:15; 5:21, 27, 34, 41; 6:12, 15; 22:30; 23:1, 6, 15, 20, 28; 24:20) and a dynamic equivalent rendering in the other four (Mt 5:22; 10:17; Mk 13:9; Lk 22:66). The NASB and ESV both opted for a dynamic equivalent rendering in all twenty-two occurrences. In just two of those cases (Mt 26:59; Mk 14:55), the ESV provided a footnote, which says, "Greek *Sanhedrin*."
[c] 1984 edition.

---

[29] See Leland Ryken, *Understanding English Bible Translation: The Case for an Essentially Literal Approach* (Wheaton, IL: Crossway, 2009), pp. 73-74. Ryken states, "To be transparent to the original text means *preserving all signposts to the ancient world* of biblical writers, as opposed to finding [modern] equivalents" (emphasis added).

The Bible uses a variety of ancient terms to measure distance, weight and monetary value. In the New Testament, we find units of money like denarius and drachma. How should translators handle these terms? Should they include them in our English versions? Or can they substitute present-day English terms like dollar, cent and penny? (In other countries, it would be words like peso, franc, mark and yen.) What have the translators of our English versions done? Let us look at some examples.

Luke 12:6 in the KJV says, "Are not five sparrows sold for two farthings?" Do you know what a farthing[30] is? It is a coin that was used in England from the thirteenth century to the twentieth. It was never used anywhere in Bible lands or in Bible times. The farthing was first minted as a coin in A.D. 1279—many centuries after the New Testament was written, and about three hundred years before the KJV was translated. The word used in Greek in Luke 12:6 is *assarion*, which was a Roman copper coin. Most English Bible readers have never heard of an *assarion* because no major English version brought this word into their translation. They all followed the pattern set by early English versions like the KJV, replacing *assarion* with a current English equivalent.[31] Most of the newer versions used "cent" or "penny."

The *kodrantēs* was another Roman coin. It was worth one quarter[32] of an *assarion*. But since the actual value was not in focus, the KJV translated it the same as *assarion* using the identical British coin, the farthing.[33] Most other English versions followed suit, translating *kodrantēs* and *assarion* the same ("cent" or "penny") even though they were not equal in value.

What about the *lepton*? Are you familiar with that one? The KJV translated it "mite." However, "mite," like "farthing," is not a biblical term. It is an old English word.[34] In Luke 12:59, the NASB, ESV and NIV translated *lepton* the same as *assarion* and *kodrantēs*. The NASB used the word *cent*, and the ESV and NIV used the word *penny*. The translators of these ver-

---

[30]*The Story of the Farthing: A Brief History*, www.chards.co.uk.
[31]WYCLIFFE translated *assarion* in this verse as *halpens* ("halfpence"); TYNDALE translated it "farthing."
[32]The words *quarter, quart* and *quadrant* all come from the same Latin origin as the word *kodrantēs*.
[33]The British word *farthing* (i.e., "fourth-ing") carries the same basic meaning as the word *quarter*.
[34]Originally, the mite was "a medieval [Dutch] copper coin of very small value." At the time of King James, the word *mite* was "used proverbially in English for 'a very small unit of money.'" Douglas Harper, Online Etymology Dictionary, www.etymonline.com.

sions knew that these coins were not equal in value; but they also knew that the actual value did not really matter. When the biblical writers used these terms, their goal was to convey a very small amount of money.[35] That is why the translators felt it was fine to translate these three different coins exactly the same in some contexts. The relative worth of *assarion, kodrantēs* and *lepton* is illustrated in figure 6.2.

In Luke 21:2, the NASB and ESV came up with an excellent meaning-based translation for the word *lepton*. Rather than translating it as a single word, they replaced it with the descriptive phrase "small copper coin."[36] There is nothing in the original text to suggest this kind of rendering. It is entirely based on the translators' knowledge of the historical meaning.

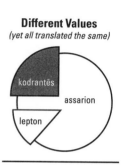

Different Values
(yet all translated the same)

kodrantēs

assarion

lepton

Fig 6.2.

There are three monetary terms in the New Testament that are used in a generic sense: *chrēma, nomisma* and *kerma,* and all three are consistently translated "coin" or "money." The words *chrysos, argyros* and *chalkos* mean "gold," "silver" and "brass."[37] These three words are sometimes used in a general sense to refer to money.

In translating the words *mina, denarius, drachma* and *statēr,* the King James translators followed their normal pattern of replacing the Roman and Greek monetary units with ordinary British coins, or other units of money familiar to their readers. When the King James translators translated units of money in the New Testament, they carefully considered their target audience—seventeenth-century citizens of England.[38] This is another example of dynamic equivalence or meaning-based translation. In the following chart (table 6.38) as with some previous charts, I have used gray shading to mark renderings that depart significantly from the form of the original. A white background indicates a more literal, transparent rendering.

---

[35]In Mk 12:42, the HCSB translated the Greek word *kodrantēs* as "[worth] very little."
[36]The NIV translated it "very small copper coin."
[37]Some versions translate *chalkos* as "copper" or "bronze" instead of "brass."
[38]See Ryken, *Understanding English Bible Translation*, pp. 74-75, under the heading "Allegiance to Audience versus Allegiance to Author."

Table 6.38

Greek	KJV	NASB	ESV	NIV
assarion	farthing	cent	penny	penny
kodrantēs	farthing	cent	penny	penny
lepton	mite	cent	penny	penny
		small copper coin	small copper coin	very small copper coin
chrēma	money	money	money	money
nomisma	money	coin	coin	coin
kerma	money	coin	coin	coin
chrysos	gold	gold	gold	gold
argyros	silver	silver	silver	silver
chalkos	brass	copper	copper	copper
mina	pound	mina	mina	mina
denarius	penny	denarius	denarius	denarius
drachma	piece of silver	silver coin	silver coin	silver coin
didrachma	tribute	two-drachma	two-drachma	two-drachma
statēr	piece of money	shekel	shekel	four-drachma
talanton	talent	talent	talent	talent

Apart from the words *gold*, *silver* and *brass*, there are twelve different terms used for money in the New Testament.[39] In every case, the KJV replaced the original Greek word with a British equivalent of that day. One of these terms, the *talent*, may appear to be a transliteration of the Greek word *talanton*, but it is not.[40] This Greek word had already migrated through classical Latin into Old English centuries before the KJV was translated. So the word *talent*, like all the rest of the KJV monetary terms, was an authentic English word. The talent was a unit of weight. There was never a coin called a talent, because it would have been far too large and heavy to carry around.[41]

In today's English, the word *talent* as a monetary unit is found only in Scripture. While "talent" is an acceptable way to translate the Greek word *talanton*, it unfortunately does not do a very good job of communicating

---

[39]Louw and Nida, *Greek-English Lexicon*, items 6.68–6.82, "Money and Monetary Units."

[40]If "talent" had been a shortened transliteration of the Greek word *talanton*, the translators of the KJV probably would have spelled it *talant*, rather than *talent,* in order to be consistent in their representation of the Greek vowels.

[41]Louw and Nida, *Greek-English Lexicon*, describe the talent as "approximately ninety pounds (English weight) or forty kilograms" (item 86.5, "Weight").

the meaning. Every first-century Greek speaker would have known that a talent (of gold or silver) was of immensely greater value than all the rest of the monetary units combined—but most English readers today are probably unaware of that fact. That is why the New Living Translation (NLT) replaced the single Greek word *talanton* with the descriptive phrase "bag of gold."[42] This is based on the same principle that the NASB, ESV and KJV used when they replaced other single words (*lepton*, *drachma* and *statēr*) with descriptive phrases like "small copper coin," "piece of silver" and "piece of money." Consider the comparison in table 6.39.

Table 6.39

Greek	English	Version
talanton	bag of gold	NLT
lepton	small copper coin	NASB, ESV
drachma	piece of silver	KJV
	silver coin	NASB, ESV
statēr	piece of money	KJV

Why did the translators of some versions choose to keep the word *talent*, even though it does not communicate the original meaning very well in English? Obviously, it is not based on a need to translate all monetary units literally. The preceding charts (tables 6.38 and 6.39) show that none of these versions did that. Apparently, the reason some versions still use the word *talent* is because of tradition and history. Almost every English-speaking Christian knows about the parable of the talents. But very few have ever heard of the *lepton* or the *kodrantēs*, so it was easy for the translators of every version to leave these terms out of their translations. Since the word *talent* is entrenched in centuries of historical tradition, it was difficult for some translators to handle *talent* the same way they handled *lepton*, *kodrantēs* and *assarion*.

Some Inconsistencies

As we noted, the KJV was consistent in the way it translated monetary units in the New Testament. In every case, the translators used seventeenth-century British coins and other monetary units of that day. But the NASB,

---

[42]*Talanton* occurs twelve times in Mt 25:15-28 and was translated "bag(s) of gold" by the NLT in each case. The only other place *talanton* occurs in the New Testament is Mt 18:24 in the phrase "10,000 talents." In this verse, the NLT translated it "millions of dollars."

ESV and NIV were not completely consistent. Sometimes they used present-day monetary terms; sometimes they did not. They translated *assarion*, *kodrantēs* and *lepton* as "cent" and "penny." But they decided to import some of the other Greek terms into English: *mina*, *denarius* and *didrachma*. I am not sure why they considered the words *mina*, *denarius* and *didrachma* more sacred than *assarion*, *kodrantēs*, *lepton* and *statēr*.

In studying New Testament monetary units, there is an interesting passage in Matthew 17 where the plot thickens. In Matthew 17:27 of this context, the Greek text uses the coin *statēr*.[43] The ESV and NASB both converted the Greek *statēr* to a Hebrew *šekel*. They could have used the Greek word *statēr*, as this would have been consistent with their pattern for translating *mina* and *denarius*. Or they could have used a meaningful equivalent like the KJV phrase "piece of money," consistent with their translation of *lepton* as "small copper coin." Instead, the NASB and ESV decided to import the Hebrew word *šekel*. The word *šekel* does not appear anywhere in the Greek New Testament, but it does appear in both the NASB and ESV translations of this verse.

There are two key points worth noting here—from Matthew's perspective and from the perspective of the NASB and ESV translators. First, some background. The actual coin in the mouth of the fish was probably a Hebrew *šekel* (not a Greek *statēr*), because a *šekel* (or half-shekel) is what the Jews would have used to pay the Jewish temple tax.

When Matthew wrote this account in the Greek language, he knew that the Greek *statēr* was virtually equivalent in value to the Hebrew *šekel*. So rather than using the name of the actual historical coin (*šekel*), he substituted the Greek word *statēr*. He knew *statēr* would be clearly understood by all his readers—not only those who were Jewish. When Matthew used the word *statēr* here, he was employing dynamic equivalence, or meaning-based, translation principles.

The NASB and ESV translators apparently felt that even though Matthew wrote the word *statēr* in the text, he did not mean *statēr*. He meant *šekel*. So they translated Matthew's thought rather than his exact word. In doing so, the NASB and ESV translators made their translations of this passage more historically accurate than the original account that Matthew wrote!

---

[43]Louw and Nida, *Greek-English Lexicon*, describe the *statēr* as "a silver coin worth two *didrachma*" (item 6.80).

I do not question the way either of these versions translated this passage. However, I do question the notion that these or any other versions are consistently literal, word-for-word or transparent to the original text. Even when they could have been literal, they often chose not to be. In this passage, the translators of the NASB and ESV incorporated their knowledge of the historical and cultural context, going beyond what could have been reasonably concluded by just reading the words of the Greek text. In this case, as in many others, the translators set aside their ideal of literal transparency in order to unearth some of the rich components of meaning that otherwise would have remained buried beneath the surface. This is the same thing that idiomatic versions do—only they do it on a more regular basis.

TRANSLATION AND INSPIRATION

The examples in this chapter clearly show that Bible translation is rarely a simple matter of finding a suitable English word to translate each Hebrew or Greek word. When we describe the connection between translation and inspiration, we cannot afford to oversimplify the issues involved. If the doctrine of verbal inspiration requires consistent word-for-word translation, then every English version is disqualified.

What Is in a Name?

In these first six chapters, we have seen many examples which prove that it is impossible for any Bible version to be literal in every context. We have also seen that the translators of every version sometimes chose not to use a literal rendering even though one was available. Therefore, I believe that some of the terminology currently used to classify Bible versions is potentially misleading—especially to the average Christian who has not studied the original languages. I will comment on a few of these terms.

Word-for-word. When Bible scholars describe an English Bible version as a word-for-word translation, they know among themselves that they do not mean that each word in English corresponds to a word in the original. But to the average reader, the term "word-for-word" could imply that translation is an exact science, almost like mathematical encryption. By now, it should be clear that there is no such thing as a consistently word-for-word translation in English.

Some versions have adopted the ideal of aiming for word-for-word renderings when it is practical to do so. But in reality, word-for-word translation is often impossible to achieve, even in the translation of any single, complete verse of Scripture. Perhaps it would be better to call these versions word-focused translations rather than word-for-word translations. This terminology would more accurately reflect the fact that matching the words of the original is merely a goal to aim for rather than reality on a broad scale.

Formal equivalence. The evidence shows that most of the forms in Hebrew and Greek do not have a truly equivalent form in English. There is a certain amount of overlap, but in many cases, the overlap is limited at best. Consistent formal equivalence in the truest sense of the term does not exist between any two languages on earth. Also, we have seen that even when there is a seemingly equivalent form available, the translators of formal equivalence versions often choose not to use it. For that reason, it would be more accurate and forthright to call it formal approximation.

Transparent. The esv translators were honest in their preface, stating that they "seek" to be transparent to the original text. In saying it this way, they clearly identified transparency as an ideal that is not always attainable. But when non-translators hear the word *transparent* (not only with the esv but also with all other literal versions) they could easily assume it is more than an ideal to aim for. The word *transparent* implies a crystal-clear window that would give a direct, virtually unclouded view into the wording of the original text. Every translator knows that this is not a reality in any version. For that reason, I think it would be less confusing and less potentially misleading to say that these versions "seek" to give a semi-transparent view into the original. That is about as close as any translation could realistically get to attaining this ideal. This terminology may even be a bit generous as there are examples on every page of every literal English version where the renderings could not be called semi-transparent.

Essentially literal. English versions that have been described as essentially literal (such as the esv[44]) do contain many essentially literal renderings. But we need to be careful when we use the term "essentially literal" as a categorical label. The word *essentially* may seem to be a bit of an overstatement. To the average

---

[44]The preface to the esv includes this statement: "The esv is an 'essentially literal' translation."

English reader who has no direct access to Hebrew or Greek, the connotation of the word *essentially* may imply a higher degree of equivalence with the original than the evidence supports. This term could carry the implication that those versions give a transparent view into "essentially" every noun, verb, tense, person, number, voice, mood and possibly even every idiom of the original. That is not true. In many cases, they do, but in many others, they do not.

It is fine for a team of translators to aim for literalness as an ideal for their particular translation. But the main problem I see with labels like word-for-word, formal equivalence, transparent to the text and essentially literal is that they focus almost exclusively on the ideal—not the real. For that reason, I prefer John Beekman and John Callow's[45] term "modified literal."[46] It contains an honest, explicit acknowledgement of the fact that the translators of every literal version have indeed made many modifications. I agree that the word *essentially* does allow for some modifications, but it seems to imply that those modifications are extremely rare.[47] With the term "modified literal," however, the word *literal* represents the ideal and the word *modified* represents the real.

Terminology for Nonliteral Versions

Some of the terms used to describe translations on the opposite end of the spectrum can be equally unclear or potentially misleading—for example, meaning-based, paraphrase and dynamic equivalence.

Meaning-based. The term "meaning-based" does an excellent job of describing the goal of translators of idiomatic versions. However, we need to be careful in the way we use this term because it could imply that translators of literal versions do not care that much about communicating meaning. That could not be further from the truth. There are countless examples that prove that the translators of every major version have embraced the principle of giving priority to meaning over form.

---

[45]John Beekman and John Callow, *Translating the Word of God* (Grand Rapids: Zondervan, 1974), p. 23.

[46]See chap. 3, "Types of Translations."

[47]This view of the word *essentially* is reflected in the following statement by Ryken: "on *extremely rare* occasions an essentially literal translation contains something other than an expression of the actual words used by the author" (*Understanding English Bible Translation*, pp. 189-90, emphasis added). Also, this statement by Grudem: "essentially literal translations will depart from complete literalness *only* where it is necessary, in cases *where a truly literal translation would make it nearly impossible* for readers *to understand the meaning*" ("Are Only *Some* Words of Scripture Breathed Out by God?" p. 24, emphasis added).

Paraphrase. The word *paraphrase* has often been used as a label for a specific class of nonliteral Bible versions.[48] When we use the word *paraphrase* in this way, however, we need to remember that paraphrasing is a translation technique that the translators of every version have used to varying degrees; as Wayne Grudem aptly stated, "every essentially literal translation has some amount of 'paraphrase.'"[49]

Dynamic (or functional) equivalence.[50] The term "dynamic equivalence" (also called functional equivalence) is potentially misleading in the same way that the term "formal equivalence" is. It would be more accurate to call it dynamic (or functional) approximation.

From this point on, for the sake of simplicity, I will primarily use the terms "modified literal" and "idiomatic" to distinguish between these two common types of Bible translations.

SUMMARY

The examples in this chapter show that even modified literal versions like the KJV, ESV and NASB do not consistently reflect the original Hebrew and Greek forms. All translations use meaning-based translation principles to varying degrees. It is not a question of whether or not translators will change the form but rather how much of the form will they try to preserve. It appears that the one thing that is truly consistent in Bible translation is the fact that it is impossible to be truly consistent.

Up to this point, we have been focusing mainly on translation examples from English Bible versions. But it would be a huge mistake to limit this discussion to English translation only. In the next chapter, we will take a peek into the vast complexity and diversity that exist in languages worldwide. To me, as a translator, it is breathtakingly beautiful. It is one more amazing testimony to the unfathomable awesomeness of our God. As we contemplate this vast world of living languages, we will open the door to another crucial body of evidence that has been largely excluded from the translation debate: the Babel factor.

---

[48]Cf. Fee and Strauss, *How to Choose a Translation*, pp. 31-32.
[49]Grudem, "Are Only *Some* Words of Scripture Breathed Out by God?," p. 23.
[50]Cf. Fee and Strauss, *How to Choose a Translation*, pp. 26-27.

7

THE BABEL FACTOR

GOD SPEAKS IN LANGUAGES
OTHER THAN ENGLISH

◆ ◆ ◆

The LORD confused the language of the whole earth;
and from there the LORD scattered them abroad
over the face of the whole earth.

GENESIS 11:9 (NASB)

In recent decades, many books and articles have been written about the ongoing debate regarding literalness in Bible translation. The common feature in most of these writings is that they focus primarily on translating the Bible into English. That is not surprising because English has more translations of Scripture than any other language in the world. But there is a problem with limiting our discussion to English translations: some of the standards that have been suggested for English Bible versions do not apply to many other languages. Therefore, it is imperative that this discussion move far beyond English translations. In this chapter, we will expand our focus to include some of the unique challenges translators face as they translate God's Word into other languages around the world.

A RADICALLY ALTERED LINGUISTIC LANDSCAPE

When God made his pronouncement at Babel, he knew one result would be that the Scriptures would have to be painstakingly translated, over and over again. He also knew it would be impossible to translate many of the original forms literally in most languages. Yet he chose to confuse the languages anyway. Obviously, God made the right choice because he always makes the right choice.

When God "confused the language of the whole earth," he did a thorough job of it. Much of the English-speaking world has no idea of the extreme diversity and complexity of languages throughout the rest of the world. Many Christians may assume that since it is possible to produce a useful, modified literal translation in English (like the KJV or NASB) it must be possible to do the same in all other languages as well. But an important piece of the puzzle has often been left out of the picture: The main reason we are able to achieve the level of literalness that exists in some English versions (especially of the New Testament) is that English and Greek are both Indo-European languages.[1] English is related to New Testament Greek.

How many times have you heard a preacher or Bible teacher mention a particular word in Greek and say, "This is the Greek word from which we get our English word _____"? I have often made that kind of statement myself—when I was teaching the Bible in English. Can you guess how many times I said that sort of thing when I was teaching in the Lamogai language? If you guessed zero, you nailed it!

When translators translate the Bible into a language of a different language family, a certain degree of literalness is still possible. For example, we have some fairly literal translations of the Old Testament in English even though Hebrew is an Afro-Asiatic language, not an Indo-European language. But as a general rule, translators are able to reach a much greater degree of literalness when translating between languages of the same language family than when translating between languages of different families.

Living Languages: 6,909

Fig. 7.1.

[1]Cf. D. A. Carson, "The Limits of Functional Equivalence in Bible Translation—and Other Limits Too," in *The Challenge of Bible Translation*, ed. Glen G. Scorgie, Mark L. Strauss and Steven M. Voth (Grand Rapids: Zondervan, 2003), p. 66.

There are currently 6,909 known living languages.[2] Only 426, or 6%, belong to the Indo-European family. (Not 6% of the population, but 6% of the living languages.) The vast majority of living languages in the world today are non-Indo-European, so they do not share the same relation to New Testament Greek that English does (see figure 7.1).

Are these 6,000-plus languages able to enjoy faithful translations of God's Word, too? Or is that a privilege reserved only for English and its Indo-European language family members? If the only faithful translation is one that is primarily word-focused like the NASB, ESV or KJV, then most of the world's languages cannot have a truly faithful translation. That would mean the majority of languages designed by God are inherently deficient, unable to communicate spiritual truth in a way that is faithful to the original.

TRANSLATING WORDS

The fact that Greek and English are both Indo-European languages does not make translation into English easy by any means. In the previous chapter, we saw some of the challenges of translating word-for-word between these distantly related cousins. But the challenge of trying to achieve word for word translation escalates sharply when we move from English to languages outside of the Indo-European family. Here is an example of mismatch between English and Lamogai words (table 7.1).

Table 7.1

Lamogai	English
karvan	today
kutu	tomorrow
kasak	the day after tomorrow
kusik	the day after the day after tomorrow
kusik laine	the day after the day after the day after tomorrow

If our goal is word-for-word translation, what single English word should we use to translate the Lamogai word *kusik* in every context? Obviously, English has no such word. This kind of mismatch is common between unrelated languages. For example, there is a single word in Vietnamese that means "someone leaves to go somewhere and something happens at home so that he

---

[2]M. Paul Lewis, ed., *Ethnologue: Languages of the World*, 16th ed. (Dallas: SIL International, 2009), www.ethnologue.com.

has to go back home."[3] In a case like this, the translator has no choice but to translate thought for thought. We have seen that the ideal goal of some translators is word-for-word translation. This ideal may sound good in theory, but it quickly breaks down when a translator tries to match words consistently from one unrelated language to another. That is the real world of translation.

Many of the languages in the Highlands of Papua New Guinea are notorious for having incredibly long words. There is one word in the Simbari language,[4] for example, that has forty-six letters:

Mabomollurolovonekumokalokwowo'jujuko'mno'juki[5]

It means "had he not delivered us." The grammar rules of Simbari make it impossible to break it down any smaller and still communicate the correct meaning. All the person markers, prefixes, suffixes and so on of this word must be connected in this way. Obviously, we would never find a single word to translate this Simbari word into English, Hebrew, Greek or any other language that is not closely related to Simbari.

Thankfully, not every word in the Simbari language is forty-six letters long. But Simbari words are characteristically much longer and carry a heavier grammatical load than English or Greek words. It is easy to see why Simbari will never have a truly usable,[6] word-focused translation like the NASB or KJV.

DEALING WITH AMBIGUITIES

One of the challenges faced by every translator is the issue of ambiguities, or double meanings. There are numerous places in Scripture where more than one meaning is possible. In many of those cases, even the Hebrew and Greek experts do not know for sure which meaning is the right one! An example of this is found in Matthew 6:13. The ambiguity is in the last part of the verse, where it says "deliver us from evil." There are two ways this phrase could be translated:

---

[3]Mildred L. Larson, *Meaning-Based Translation: A Guide to Cross-Language Equivalence*, rev. ed. (Lanham, MD: University Press of America, 1998), p. 7.

[4]Contributed by David Ogg, NTM, Papua New Guinea.

[5]The apostrophes ['] in this word do not indicate contraction, as they would in English. The apostrophe symbol in Simbari represents a phonetic sound called the glottal stop. This sound is not assigned its own letter in English.

[6]By "usable," I mean one that is understandable to the average reader. We know from previous examples that excessive word-for-word literalness can cloud the meaning in English. The likelihood of distorting the meaning in this way is even greater when translating into a language that is not related to *koine* Greek.

1. deliver us *from evil*

2. deliver us *from the evil one*

These two options are not based on differences in the Greek manuscripts but on genuine ambiguity in the Greek text. Every translator is forced to make a choice—not arbitrarily, but carefully. Here is how several English versions translated this phrase (table 7.2).

Table 7.2

Matthew 6:13			
KJV:	*deliver us from evil*	NKJV:	*deliver us from the evil one*
NASB:	*deliver us from evil*	ASV:	*deliver us from the evil one*
RSV:	*deliver us from evil*	NRSV:	*rescue us from the evil one*
ESV:	*deliver us from evil*	HCSB:	*deliver us from the evil one*

There are many genuine ambiguities in Scripture, but that does not mean God was not sure what he meant to say in those contexts. Nor does it mean that the original readers did not understand the meaning of what was written. The original New Testament readers spoke a living *koine* Greek language.[7] Therefore, they had a huge advantage over anyone today who attempts to learn *koine* Greek solely from the pages of a book.

Every translator must deal with the ambiguities that exist in Scripture,[8] but translators who translate into non-Indo-European languages have to deal with many more ambiguities than those who have translated into English. As long as the debate about Bible translation stays within the realm of English translation, the tendency will be to oversimplify some of the issues. I believe that many well-meaning Christians have unwittingly made English the ultimate standard.

In the remaining pages of this chapter, we will look at a few of the many kinds of interpretive decisions translators often face when translating the New Testament into a non-Indo-European language. My purpose in pointing out these examples is to help us move beyond exalting English as the ultimate standard for discussing translation issues.

---

[7] New Testament Greek is considered a dead language because it is no longer used as the primary means of communication within a currently existing human society.

[8] Cf. D. A. Carson, *The King James Version Debate: A Plea for Realism* (Grand Rapids: Baker Book House, 1979), p. 88. He states, "even in the most 'literal' of translations, the translator must on occasion make decisions as to the meaning of a passage."

THE GENITIVE CONSTRUCTION IN GREEK

We have all been told that New Testament Greek is a precise language. That is true in some areas of the language, but it is not true of the genitive construction.[9] The genitive in Greek is commonly used to show simple possession, and in those cases, it is straightforward. But in other contexts, the Greek genitive often has two or more possible meanings. An example of this is found in 1 Thessalonians 1:3 (NASB): "constantly bearing in mind your work of faith and labor of love and steadfastness of hope in our Lord Jesus Christ." The three genitives I would like to focus on in this verse are

- work of faith
- labor of love
- steadfastness of hope

In Lamogai, a literal translation of these three phrases would sound like nonsense. For example, the phrase "labor of love" would sound like "labor that is possessed by love." And "steadfastness of hope" would sound like "steadfastness owned by hope."

Obviously, love cannot possess labor, and hope cannot be the owner of steadfastness. That means in order to translate this verse into Lamogai, the translator needs to dig a bit deeper to find out what these phrases mean. This is where the ambiguity of the Greek genitive comes into play because each of these three phrases has more than one possible meaning.

The first one, "work of faith,"[10] is less ambiguous than the other two. Most commentators agree that this phrase means their work was a result of their faith in God.

The next, "labor of love," is less clear. It could mean any of these three possibilities:[11]

1. They labor because of *God's* love for *them*.
2. They labor because of *their* love for *God*.
3. They labor because of *their* love for *others*.

---

[9]Cf. Gordon D. Fee and Mark L. Strauss, *How to Choose a Translation for All Its Worth* (Grand Rapids: Zondervan, 2007), pp. 77-83.

[10]See also 2 Thess 1:11.

[11]These three options are not the only possible interpretations for this phrase.

In Lamogai, it is impossible to come up with a single statement that would include all three of these meanings. The grammar of Lamogai forces the translator to make a choice—just as English grammar forces every English version to choose between "evil" and "the evil one" in Matthew 6:13.

The third genitive phrase, "steadfastness of hope," is probably the most ambiguous of the three. Translators and commentators seem to be split evenly between the following two interpretations:

1. They were steadfast in continuing to hope for the return of Jesus Christ.

2. They were steadfast in their Christian walk because of their hope in Jesus Christ.

In other words, either their hope is steadfast (option 1), or else their hope causes steadfastness (option 2). The only way to translate this phrase into Lamogai is to choose one of these two interpretations. It is required by the grammar of Lamogai and many other languages.

In English, we are not forced to make such a choice. That is why many versions translated it "steadfastness of hope." Most idiomatic versions, however, made an interpretive choice rather than leaving it ambiguous. The following chart (table 7.3) shows how several idiomatic versions reflected these two interpretations.

Table 7.3

1	Their hope was steadfast	2	Their hope caused steadfast endurance in their lives
NLT	your continual anticipation of the return of our Lord Jesus Christ	PHILLIPS	the hope that you have in our Lord Jesus Christ means sheer dogged endurance in the life that you live
TEV	your hope in our Lord Jesus Christ is firm	NIV	your endurance inspired by hope in our Lord Jesus Christ
CEV	your firm hope in our Lord Jesus Christ	NCV	you continue to be strong because of your hope in our Lord Jesus Christ

On one hand, it might be safer for a translator to leave this phrase ambiguous because we do not know for sure which meaning Paul intended. On the other hand, if hundreds or even thousands of other languages require that an interpretive choice be made, is it wrong to do the same thing in some English versions? If preserving the ambiguity of the Greek genitive were a requirement of faithfulness and accuracy, wouldn't God have made sure that every language in the world was capable of fulfilling that requirement?

As it turns out, every modified literal version in English preserved the ambiguity[12] of the phrase "steadfastness of hope." Yet I find it interesting that most Bible teachers and Bible commentators seem to teach just one meaning to the exclusion of the other. The following chart (table 7.4) lists the interpretative position taken by a few recognized Bible teachers and commentators.

Table 7.4

Their hope was steadfast	Their hope caused endurance in their lives
John MacArthur[a]	J. Vernon McGee[b]
John Piper[c]	John R. W. Stott[d]
Ray C. Stedman[e]	John Walvoord and Roy Zuck[f]
Matthew Henry[g]	William Hendrickson[h]
William MacDonald[i]	Leon Morris[j]
R. C. H. Lenski[k]	Jamieson, Fausset and Brown[l]
Paul Ellingsworth and Eugene Nida[m]	Albert Barnes[n]
F. F. Bruce[o]	Robert L. Thomas[p]

[a] John MacArthur, *The MacArthur New Testament Commentary 1 and 2 Thessalonians* (Chicago: Moody Press, 2002), pp. 18-20; *The Certainty of the Second Coming* (Panorama City, CA: Grace to You, 2005-2006).
[b] J. Vernon McGee, *Notes and Outlines [on] 1 and 2 Thessalonians* (Pasadena, CA: Thru the Bible Radio Network).
[c] John Piper, *When I Don't Desire God* (Wheaton, IL: Crossway, 2004), p. 100.
[d] John R. W. Stott, *The Message of Thessalonians* (Leicester: Inter-Varsity Press, 1991), p. 30.
[e] Ray C. Stedman, *Changed Lives* (Palo Alto, CA: Discovery Publishing, 1987).
[f] John F. Walvoord and Roy B. Zuck, eds., *The Bible Knowledge Commentary: An Exposition of the Scriptures by Dallas Seminary Faculty* (Wheaton, IL: Victor Books, 1983).
[g] Matthew Henry, *Matthew Henry's Commentary on the Whole Bible* (Wilmington, DE: Sovereign Grace Publishers, 1972), p. 1171.
[h] William Hendrickson, *Exposition of I and II Thessalonians*, New Testament Commentary (Grand Rapids: Baker, 1955), p. 48.
[i] William MacDonald, *Believer's Bible Commentary* (Nashville: Thomas Nelson, 1990), pp. 839-40.
[j] Leon Morris, *The First and Second Epistles to the Thessalonians*, New International Commentary on the New Testament (Grand Rapids: Eerdmans, 1991).
[k] R. C. H. Lenski, *The Interpretation of St. Paul's Epistles to the Colossians, to the Thessalonians, to Timothy, to Titus and to Philemon* (Minneapolis: Augsburg, 1946).
[l] Robert Jamieson, A. R. Fausset and David Brown, *Commentary Critical and Explanatory on the Whole Bible* (New York: George H. Doran Company, 1871).
[m] Paul Ellingsworth and Eugene A. Nida, *A Translator's Handbook on Paul's Letters to the Thessalonians* (New York: United Bible Societies, 1976).
[n] Albert Barnes, *Barnes' Notes on the New Testament* (Grand Rapids: Kregel, 1962), p. 1083.
[o] F. F. Bruce, *1 and 2 Thessalonians*, Word Biblical Commentary 45 (Waco, TX: Word, 1982).
[p] Robert L. Thomas, "1 Thessalonians," in *The Expositor's Bible Commentary*, ed. Frank E. Gaebelein (Grand Rapids: Zondervan, 1978), p. 241.

These Bible teachers and Bible commentators seem to treat the ambiguous phrase "steadfastness of hope" as though it only had one meaning. In most cases, they do not even mention the fact that there is another possible interpre-

---

[12] As noted above, the issue is perceived ambiguity of us as readers, not intended ambiguity of the original author.

tation. It is fine for a teacher to handle it that way, yet it does seem to call into question the value of preserving the ambiguity in translation. The reason translators preserve this kind of ambiguity is to avoid excluding either interpretation, so both meanings can be taught, leaving the interpretation up to the reader.

I am not criticizing any of these Bible teachers or commentators for making a clear-cut, interpretive choice here. As a translator, I made one also. I had to. That is the only way I could translate this verse into Lamogai. I did not make my decision lightly. I based it on careful study of the context—not only the immediate context of this chapter but also the broader context including both letters to the Thessalonians and the passages in the book of Acts that describe Paul's ministry at Thessalonica. This same kind of interpretive decision will likely be necessary in many other non-Indo-European languages as well.

Table 7.5

	Literal Wording[a]		Interpretive Rendering
Rev 16:5[b]	*the angel of the waters*	ESV	the angel **in charge of** the waters
Rom 9:31[c]	*a law of righteousness*	ESV	a law **that would lead** to righteousness
Rom 15:5[d]	*the God of perseverance*	NASB	the God **who gives** perseverance

[a] According to footnotes in the ESV and NASB.
[b] This phrase was translated literally as "angel of the waters" in the NASB, HCSB, KJV, NKJV and others.
[c] This phrase was translated literally as "law of righteousness" in the NASB, KJV, NKJV and others.
[d] This phrase was translated literally as "God of endurance/patience" in the ESV, HCSB, KJV, NKJV and others.

Word-focused translations such as the ESV and NASB usually translate Greek genitives literally—but not always. Sometimes, these versions have chosen to interpret the underlying meaning rather than translating the genitive literally (see table 7.5). The ESV and NASB translators determined, at least in these cases, that it is acceptable to set aside the literal wording of the Greek genitive and provide an expanded interpretation in its place.

OLDER BROTHER—YOUNGER BROTHER

Some languages, including Lamogai, have two different words for brother: one means "older brother," and the other means "younger brother." In many cases, these languages do not have a generic word that includes both.[13] Relating this to translation, which of the sons of Zebedee do you think was older,

---

[13] The Lamogai translation sometimes imports the Melanesian Pidgin term *brata* to refer to older and younger siblings collectively, but there is no Lamogai word that carries this meaning.

James or John? The Bible does not tell us, but there are some clues. The names James and John occur together about twenty times in the New Testament. In every occurrence, James is named first. Since there is not much else to go on, most translators who have faced this issue have considered that to be enough evidence to say James must be the older brother. Here is how we translated this pair of names in Matthew 17:1 in the Lamogai New Testament:[14]

Jems akap ino tikino Jon
James along-with his younger-brother John

PRONOUNS

Another area where the Lamogai language functions differently from English and Greek is in its pronouns. Lamogai does not have any masculine or feminine pronouns. Every pronoun in Lamogai is gender neutral. For example, the Lamogai pronoun [*ye*] means either "he" or "she," and the pronoun [*-e*] means either "him" or "her."[15] In translation, this forced us to deal with ambiguities that English translators did not face. One example is in Matthew 2:11. The potentially problematic pronoun in this case is "him" (Gk *autō*) at the end of the sentence: "going into the house they saw the child with Mary his mother, and they fell down and worshiped him" (ESV). The closest word-for-word rendering of this statement in Lamogai would mean "they saw the child with Mary his mother, and they fell down and worshiped him/her." Obviously, this kind of word-for-word rendering would create a serious ambiguity. The reader would be left wondering whether the worshippers fell down and worshipped "him" (the child) or "her" (Mary). In order to eliminate the ambiguity, we had to translate it like this: "they fell down and worshipped the child."

ABSTRACT NOUNS

English, like its Indo-European cousin Greek, seems to have a deep fondness for nouns, while many other languages and cultures around the world (including Lamogai) are much more verb-centered.[16] Lamogai primarily uses

---

[14]The same is true of sisters like Mary and Martha. The translator must determine who is older.
[15]Or "it."
[16]Cf. Eugene A. Nida, *Bible Translating* (London: United Bible Societies, 1947), pp. 246-50. See also John Beekman and John Callow, *Translating the Word of God* (Grand Rapids: Zondervan, 1974), p. 26; James D. Smith III, "Faith as Substance or Surety," in *The Challenge of Bible*

nouns to refer to things we can see, hear, taste, smell, touch or talk to. But English and Greek often use nouns to represent actions, events, processes, feelings, experiences and descriptions. For example, English uses the abstract nouns "freedom," "bravery" and "happiness." There are many abstract nouns in the Bible such as "love," "salvation," "faith," "grace" and "justification." In many languages, these concepts do not exist in noun form, so they must be communicated using verbs and other parts of speech. The Lamogai language does have some abstract nouns, but even the ones that do exist are not used very often. If we were to try to match every abstract noun in Greek with a noun in Lamogai, it would not only sound unnatural, it would also be impossible to understand.

Because English and Greek are related languages, the translation of abstract nouns is usually not a problem for us. Most Greek nouns can be translated fairly literally into English without sacrificing meaning or even naturalness. But in a language like Lamogai, it is another story. The fact that Lamogai has very few abstract nouns is only one of the challenges faced by the translator. There are other factors that further complicate the matter. As an example, let us consider that simple little thing called "love."

A Translator Trying to Cope with "Love"

What is love? Love is not something I can have a conversation with or put in my back pocket and carry around with me. Love, in its truest sense, is an action that I do for someone or a feeling of affection that I experience toward someone. Therefore, in many languages, it is impossible to convey the idea of "love" using a noun.

In Lamogai, "love" is always a verb. Also, anytime we talk about love in the Lamogai language, we are required by the grammar to specify both who is doing the loving and whom they are loving. It is impossible to talk about love in Lamogai without including this information. Therefore, when we translated the statement "love is patient" (1 Cor 13:4) into Lamogai, it was not quite as simple as translating it into English. The first question I had to ask in translating this verse was Who loves whom? There are three possibilities:

Translation, ed. Glen G. Scorgie, Mark L. Strauss and Steven M. Voth (Grand Rapids: Zondervan, 2003), p. 390, quote by Eugene Loos.

- God loves people

- People love God

- People love people

Obviously, the original meaning could include more than just one of these options. But in order to translate this verse into Lamogai, I had to decide which of these three possibilities is the primary focus. This type of translational choice cannot be taken lightly. As a translator, I had to thoroughly study the context and carefully weigh every option. There are two blanks that I needed to fill in here:

<u>___?___</u> love(s) <u>___?___</u>
(who)   (whom)

Consider the first blank. "Who" is supposed to show love in this passage? The best way to figure this out is to look at the context. Let us read 1 Corinthians 13:1-3 (NET):

> If I speak in the tongues of men and of angels, but I do not have love, I am a noisy gong or a clanging cymbal. And if I have prophecy, and know all mysteries and all knowledge, and if I have all faith so that I can remove mountains, but do not have love, I am nothing. If I give away everything I own, and if I give over my body in order to boast, but do not have love, I receive no benefit.

Paul's repeated use of the pronoun "I" makes it clear that he is including himself in the exhortation of this passage. Obviously, Paul is a person, so it seems reasonable that we would fill in the first blank with the word *people*.

<u>People</u> love <u>___?___</u>
(who)   (whom)

What about the second blank? Whom are we people supposed to love? Again, the answer is in the context. Here is what it says in 1 Corinthians 13:4-5 (NIV):

> Love is patient, love is kind. It does not envy, it does not boast, it is not proud. It does not dishonor others, it is not self-seeking, it is not easily angered, it keeps no record of wrongs.

When do we most often exercise qualities like patience, kindness, boastfulness, pride and anger? It is usually in our relationship with other people. Therefore, it seems apparent from these verses that the second blank should be the same as the first. The main focus of this passage is on people loving people. Here is one possible way the phrase "love is patient" could be translated into a language like Lamogai: "The person who loves people acts patiently toward people."

I realize that a rendering like this may bother some; but in many languages, the only alternative would be to translate this phrase in a way that would result in pure nonsense. God could have designed every language on earth to use abstract nouns in the same way Greek does, but he chose not to, so we must conclude that he allows us to use other means to convey his meaning.

Obviously, this is only one of many places where Greek uses a noun to express the idea of love.[17] Other verses may be even more difficult to translate than this one. For example, 1 John 4:8 and 1 John 4:16 say, "God is love." A literal translation of this phrase into Lamogai would be something like, "God is his insides going toward." This literal statement sounds just as ridiculous in Lamogai as it does in English.

As I wrestled with these and other complex translation issues, I was reminded of the eternal truth that God is sovereign, and nothing he does is random. God is the one who divinely inspired the phrases "love is patient" and "God is love." Yet this same God created the Lamogai language (along with many other languages) in such a way that it cannot come remotely close to reflecting these phrases literally.

A Monolingual Perspective

I have my own theory on why there is often disagreement among English-speaking Christians about Bible translations. I believe it is in part due to the fact that most of us live in monolingual societies. The majority of native English speakers have never learned a second living language to full fluency. And of those who have, most learned another Indo-European language[18]—which of course, would be related in some ways to English. Many English

---

[17]There are more than 125 places in the New Testament where a Greek noun is translated "love" in English.

[18]For a complete listing of Indo-European languages, living and dead, see www.ethnologue.com.

speakers base their view of New Testament translation entirely on translating from Greek into its Indo-European relative, English. I believe this narrow perspective is a major reason for many of the disagreements that exist regarding English translations.

We cannot afford to leave the Babel factor out of the translation equation. If we do, we will be forced to rely on incomplete information; and incomplete information will inevitably produce incomplete and faulty conclusions. As we seek to determine what practices are acceptable in translation, we need to include the evidence that exists in *all* living languages of the world, far beyond the boundaries of English.

But it does not end there. There is another body of evidence that is sometimes overlooked in the ongoing discussions about translation. Beneath the surface of the Scriptures themselves lie clues that can help us more clearly understand the translation process. In the next chapter, we will examine some of these clues, adding them to the evidence we have considered up to this point. Let the Scriptures speak!

8

First-Century Translators

Setting Precedents for
Future Translators

◆ ◆ ◆

We hear them speaking in our own languages
about the great deeds God has done!

ACTS 2:11 (NET)

A Divinely Sanctioned Venture

As we surge into the twenty-first century there is more translation taking
place between languages worldwide than ever before. But translating
written text from one language to another is not a new endeavor by any
means. Historians tell us that translation of the ancient Hebrew Scriptures
into Greek began almost three hundred years before the time of Christ.
This Greek translation of the Old Testament in its various forms is called
the Septuagint.[1]

Translating the Scriptures into another language was not merely a human
idea. God put his stamp of approval on it when he prompted the writers of
the Greek New Testament to quote or translate verses from the Hebrew Old
Testament. Also, when Jesus commanded his followers to "go and make

---

[1]The Septuagint is often symbolized by the Roman numeral LXX (seventy).

disciples of all nations" (Mt 28:19 NIV) he knew it would be necessary to translate the Scriptures into the languages of those many nations. Since God endorses the translation of his Word into other languages, he no doubt understands the linguistic barriers and certainly has some standards in mind for translating Scripture in an acceptable way.

TRANSLATION WITHIN THE NEW TESTAMENT

The civilized world in the first century A.D. used a variety of languages. Jesus and his followers spoke Aramaic. Hebrew was used alongside of Aramaic in the synagogues. The *lingua franca* of the Roman Empire was *koine* Greek, yet the ethnic Romans still retained their own language, Latin (see Jn 19:20). Some of the other Gentile people groups to whom the gospel was introduced continued to use their indigenous languages as well (see Acts 14:11). Needless to say, there was a lot of translation taking place in governmental, commercial and other practical contexts.

There are many New Testament examples of speech translated from one language to another. The discourses of Jesus and his disciples took place in the Aramaic language, but since the New Testament was written in Greek, all those discourses had to be translated by the Gospel writers. The Old Testament was mostly written in Hebrew, so every time an Old Testament verse was quoted in the New Testament, it too had to be translated into Greek. In some cases, the New Testament authors apparently quoted the Septuagint translation. In other cases, they may have composed their own Greek translation directly from Hebrew. Even though there are no translation standards prescribed in Scripture, there are translation standards exemplified in Scripture.

We read this important statement in 2 Peter 1:21 (NASB): "no prophecy was ever made by an act of human will, but men moved by the Holy Spirit spoke from God." In the context of Peter's epistle, this verse applies primarily to the ancient prophets who were the writers of the Old Testament. But the same principle holds true for the apostles and prophets who wrote the New Testament. Those human authors, "moved by the Holy Spirit," sometimes became human translators. Just as the Holy Spirit guided them in authoring the New Testament, so he guided them in translating verses from the Old Testament. In their dual role as authors and translators, they made no mistakes because none of their writings was an act of human will.

The translational choices of these divinely appointed translators were not merely tolerated by God; they were endorsed by him—even initiated by him—as he breathed his holy Word through these men. Sometimes, their Greek translation of Old Testament verses followed the Hebrew manuscripts as we have them today, but not in every case.

In this chapter, we will look at a few translational renderings of first-century authors like Paul, James and Matthew. But before we discuss the verses that illustrate translation, let us look at the words in Greek that describe translation.

To "Translate" in Greek

There are three main Greek verbs for "translate" used in the New Testament. All three are closely related to each other in form and are virtually identical in the ways they are used in Scripture. The most basic of the three is *hermēneuō*.[2] This is the Greek word from which we get our English word *hermeneutics*, which theologians use to describe the theory and methodology of Bible interpretation. Our English versions usually render this word as either "translate" or "interpret." Here are some examples (table 8.1).

Table 8.1

	NASB	KJV
Jn 1:42	Cephas (which is **translated** Peter)	Cephas, which by **interpretation**, A stone
Jn 9:7	Siloam (which is **translated**, Sent)	Siloam, (which is by **interpretation**, Sent)
Heb 7:2	by the **translation** . . . King of Righteousness	by **interpretation** King of Righteousness

The related Greek word *diermēneuō* is also rendered "translate" or "interpret" in some contexts (table 8.2).

Table 8.2

	NASB	NKJV	ESV
Acts 9:36	Tabitha (which **translated** in Greek is called Dorcas)	Tabitha, which is **translated**, Dorcas	Tabitha, which **translated**, means Dorcas
1 Cor 12:30	All do not speak with tongues, do they? All do not **interpret**, do they?	Do all speak with tongues? Do all **interpret**?	Do all speak with tongues? Do all **interpret**?

[2]The other two related Greek verbs for "translate" are compound forms of *hermēneuō* with contracted prepositional prefixes: *diermēneuō* (*dia* + *hermēneuō*) and *methermēneuō* (*meta* + *hermēneuō*).

The area of meaning of *diermēneuō* is developed further in Luke 24:27, where some versions translated it "explain" or "expound" (table 8.3).[3]

Table 8.3

NASB	NKJV
Lk 24:27 He **explained** to them the things concerning Himself in all the Scriptures	He **expounded** to them in all the Scriptures the things concerning Himself.

It should come as no surprise that the area of meaning of these three Greek words (figure 8.1) includes both "translating" (from one language to another) and "interpreting" (i.e., explaining, expounding). We have seen several examples in previous chapters which show that all translation involves some interpretation.[4]

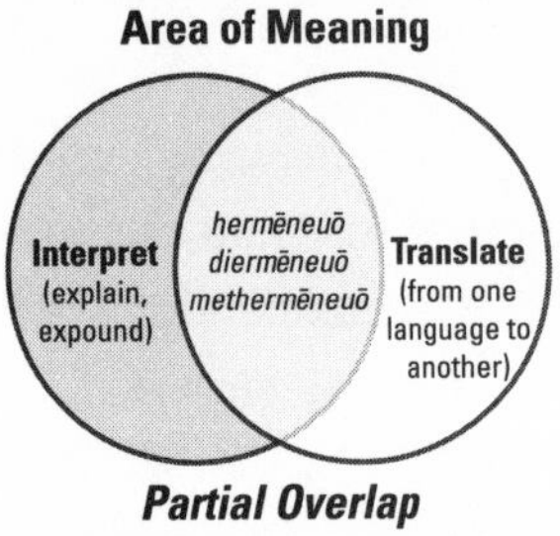

Let us look at a few examples of translation within the New Testament.

Area of Meaning

Interpret (explain, expound) — *hermēneuō* *diermēneuō* *methermēneuō* — Translate (from one language to another)

Partial Overlap

Fig. 8.1.

NAMES IN THE NEW TESTAMENT

How should proper names be translated in Scripture? For example, if the original says Abram, would it be acceptable to translate it Abraham instead? Or if the original says the LORD, could it be changed to God? This is not a trick question. As a translation consultant working with other translators, I would expect them to translate Abram as Abram, and Abraham as Abraham. And if the original says "the LORD," I would expect them to translate it "the LORD," not "God." But it seems like I may be more particular about consistently translating proper names than some biblical authors were. For example, in Romans 4:3, the apostle Paul quoted Genesis 15:6 in this way: "what does the Scripture say? 'Abraham believed God, and it was credited to him as righteousness.'"[5]

---

[3] The ESV translated it "interpret" in this verse.

[4] Cf. Gordon D. Fee and Mark L. Strauss, *How to Choose a Translation for All Its Worth* (Grand Rapids: Zondervan, 2007), pp. 30-31. See also Daniel B. Wallace, *NET, NIV, ESV: A Brief Historical Comparison* (The Biblical Studies Foundation, 2008, www.bible.org). In this article, Wallace wrote, "all translations are interpretive."

[5] NASB. See also Gal 3:6 and Jas 2:23.

The Septuagint, which Paul was apparently quoting here, says Abram[6] instead of Abraham. That makes sense—because the Lord did not give him the name Abraham until many years after the events of Genesis 15. But in Romans 4:3, Paul changed it from Abram to Abraham, even though he introduced this quote by saying, "what does the Scripture say?" This phrase is similar to the one commonly used by Jesus: "it is written."

If you compare Genesis 15:6 with what Paul wrote in Romans 4:3, you will notice another name change: "the LORD" is changed to "God." This time, Paul cannot be held responsible. It appears that he was quoting the Septuagint (or the Hebrew text underlying it), which says "God," but the Hebrew text that our English versions are based on says "the LORD."[7] There is no way to know for sure when or how this name change came about. In any case, God allowed it sometime between the writing of Genesis and the translation of the Old and New Testaments into English.

Paul was not the only one to make this kind of name substitution. James and Peter both changed "the LORD" to "God" when they quoted Proverbs 3:34 (table 8.4).[8]

Table 8.4

Proverbs 3:34	James 4:6 and 1 Peter 5:5
The **LORD** resists the proud, but gives grace to the humble[a]	**God** opposes the proud, but gives grace to the humble[b]

[a] LXX.
[b] ESV.

The author of the book of Hebrews also substituted "God" for "the LORD" in Hebrews 9:20, quoting Exodus 24:8 like this (table 8.5).[9]

Table 8.5

Exodus 24:8	Hebrews 9:20
The blood of the covenant that the **LORD** has made with you	The blood of the covenant that **God** commanded for you

---

[6] The Hebrew (*BHS*) says "he." Clearly, the antecedent of "he" is "Abram" from Gen 15:1, 2, 3.
[7] The Hebrew word used here is sometimes transliterated in English as Jehovah or Yahweh. There is no Greek equivalent for this name, but the New Testament writers consistently translated it *kyrios* ("Lord") when quoting the Old Testament Scriptures. This is apparently based on the LXX translation of Jehovah/Yahweh as *kyrios* ("Lord").
[8] The LXX translation of this verse says "Lord" (*kyrios*). The Hebrew (*BHS*) says "he," but the antecedent is clearly "LORD" (Jehovah/Yahweh) from the previous verse (Prov 3:33).
[9] ESV.

Does it really matter if we change Abram to Abraham, or say "God" instead of "the LORD"? Apparently not, because God allowed it in Romans 4:3. The form has been changed, but the meaning is the same. Abram is Abraham, even though he was not yet called that in Genesis 15. Also, the LORD is God, and God is the LORD. God in his sovereignty allowed New Testament authors to quote Genesis 15:6 and other passages in a form that is not a word-for-word translation of the verses from which they originated.

WALKING OR SITTING?

In describing the beginning of Jesus' earthly ministry (Mt 4:12-17), Matthew quoted Isaiah 9:1-2, which says the Gentiles "walk in darkness." But in quoting these verses, Matthew changed the word *walk* to "sit"[10] in Matthew 4:16 (table 8.6). He made it clear that he was quoting Scripture by saying, "This was to fulfill what was spoken through Isaiah the prophet" (Mt 4:14 NASB).

Table 8.6

Isaiah 9:2	Matthew 4:16
The people who **walk** in darkness[a]	The people who **sit** in darkness[b]

[a] NASB.
[b] NET.

The Greek language would have allowed Matthew to translate this phrase "the people who walk in darkness." That is how the Greek Septuagint translated Isaiah 9:2. Also, the idea of people walking in spiritual darkness is used elsewhere in the Greek New Testament. For example, John 8:12 says, "Whoever follows me will not walk in darkness" (ESV).[11]

When Matthew changed the phrase "walk in darkness" to "sit in darkness," did he distort "what was spoken through Isaiah the prophet"? Obviously not, because God inspired Matthew's writings, just as he inspired Isaiah's. The real focus of this passage is not on the act of walking or the posture of sitting; it is on the state of existing in spiritual darkness. So changing the verb from "walk" to "sit" does not affect the underlying meaning—it affects only the form.

---

[10] The phrase "sit in darkness" occurs other places in the Old Testament, but not in Is 9:2 (see Ps 107:10; Is 42:7; Mic 7:8). This phrase is also quoted in Lk 1:79.

[11] See also Jn 12:35 and 1 Jn 1:6. In these three verses, John used a different Greek word for "walk" than the LXX used in Is 9:2, but the meaning is the same.

In translating Matthew 4:16, most modified literal versions chose to use a semi-transparent rendering like "sit" or "sat,"[12] but some versions opted for a more meaning-based, idiomatic translation. For example, the ESV translated it "the people dwelling in darkness."[13] The figurative rendering "dwell" is certainly acceptable. In fact, from a meaning-based perspective, "dwell" may do a better job of capturing the underlying thought intended by the author in this context.

The word Matthew used here is *kathēmai*, the most common Greek word for "sit" in the New Testament. Every Greek-English lexicon lists "sit" as the primary meaning of this word. And "sit" is by far the most common translation of this word in modified literal versions. (The KJV translated it "sit," or a variation thereof, in eighty-eight of its eighty-nine occurrences.) So "sit" is presumably the most transparent rendering of the Greek word *kathēmai*.[14] But apparently the actual word does not matter, because Matthew felt free to change Isaiah's word from "walk" to "sit," and the ESV felt free to change Matthew's word from "sit" to "dwell" (table 8.7).

Table 8.7

Isaiah	Matthew	ESV
Walk in darkness	**Sit** in darkness	**Dwell** in darkness

ACTIVE OR PASSIVE?

When the apostle Paul quoted Genesis 15:6, we saw that there were two name changes from the Hebrew: Abraham and God. But there is another change in this quote. The last clause is changed from active to passive voice. Paul was apparently quoting the Septuagint, which uses a passive construction here, but the Hebrew text that our English versions are based on uses an active construction (table 8.8).[15]

---

[12]E.g., NASB, KJV, NKJV, RSV, NRSV, ASV, YLT and others.
[13]The HCSB translated it "the people who live in darkness."
[14]Word-focused versions such as the NASB generally consider "sit" to be the most literal rendering of *kathēmai*, as confirmed in Rev 14:6, where the NASB translated *kathēmai* as "live" and provided the footnote, "Lit *sit*."
[15]ESV.

Table 8.8

Genesis 15:6 *(active)*	Romans 4:3 *(passive)*
"he counted it to him as righteousness."	"it was counted to him as righteousness."

Table 8.9 is another example.[16]

Table 8.9

Isaiah 25:8 *(active)*	1 Corinthians 15:54 *(passive)*
"He will swallow up death in victory."	"Death is swallowed up in victory."

Some translators have felt obligated to try to match every passive construction in the original with a passive, and every active with an active. Apparently, that is not a requirement of faithfulness and accuracy in translation because Old Testament verses quoted in the New do not all measure up to this standard.

JESUS QUOTING SCRIPTURE

When Jesus was on earth, he often quoted verses from the Old Testament by saying, "It is written." Sometimes the wording of his quotes followed the Hebrew text as we have it today; sometimes it followed the Septuagint (or the Hebrew text beneath it); and sometimes it followed the Aramaic oral paraphrase of that time, which was later put into writing as the Targum.[17]

Matthew 4:9-10 records the following conversation between the devil and the Lord Jesus. The word we will be focusing on is "worship":

> [the devil] said to [Jesus], "All these I will give you, if you will fall down and worship me." Then Jesus said to him, "Be gone, Satan! For it is written, 'You shall worship the Lord your God and him only shall you serve.'"[18]

When Jesus quoted Deuteronomy 6:13[19] here, he made a word substitution that is not visible in most English versions.[20] But it would have

---

[16]KJV.

[17]Cf. Craig A. Evans, "The Scriptures of Jesus and His Earliest Followers," in *The Canon Debate*, ed. Lee Martin McDonald and James A. Sanders (Peabody, MA: Hendrickson, 2002).

[18]ESV.

[19]Also Deut 10:20.

[20]Jesus' word substitution in this verse is reflected in *Young's Literal Translation*.

jumped off the page to many first-century Jewish readers who were familiar with the Hebrew Scriptures. Two common Hebrew words used for "worship" in the Old Testament are *yārē'*, which means "fear," and *šāḥāh*, which means "bow down." Greek also uses "fear" (*phobeomai*) and "bow down" (*proskyneō*) to speak of worship. The verse in Deuteronomy that Jesus quoted here uses the Hebrew word for "fear." But when he quoted it to the devil, he changed it to the word for "bow down." This is what Jesus said: "It has been written, you shall *bow in worship* to the Lord your God . . . only." But that is not the way it had "been written." The verse in Deuteronomy says "you shall *fear*" the Lord. It does not say "you shall *bow in worship*" to the Lord. Of course, both words are used to mean "worship," so Jesus did not change the meaning; he only changed the word. I believe Jesus made this switch for a specific reason. Here is a summary of this part of the dialogue:

> Satan said: "fall down and *bow in worship* to me"
>
> Jesus said: "It is written, ' . . . you shall *bow in worship* to the Lord . . . only'"
>
> Deuteronomy 6:13 says: "you shall *fear* the LORD . . . only"

Jesus intentionally changed the original word *fear* to match the particular phrase "bow down" used by the devil in this conversation. The actual form of the word did not seem to matter to him as long as it carried the same basic meaning (i.e., worship). In so quoting this verse, Jesus used a dynamic equivalence approach to translation; he expressed the thought, not the actual word. Could it be that we are more concerned about translating the form of the original words than the Lord himself is?

Most of the time when Jesus quoted the Old Testament Scriptures, he did not change the words. But even this single occurrence seems to indicate that he considered this kind of change acceptable in certain contexts.

EVERY JOT AND TITTLE

Before moving on, I would like to look at one more statement of Jesus recorded in Scripture. It is a statement that has sometimes been used to suggest that Jesus supports form-based translation only.[21] In Matthew 5:18

---

[21]See Wayne Grudem, "Are Only *Some* Words of Scripture Breathed Out by God? Why Plenary Inspiration Favors 'Essentially Literal' Bible Translation," in C. John Collins, Wayne

(KJV) Jesus said this: "verily I say unto you, Till heaven and earth pass, one jot or one tittle shall in no wise pass from the law, till all be fulfilled."

What did Jesus mean by this statement? Was he suggesting that a faithful translation of God's Word must reflect every jot and tittle of the original form? We have seen enough evidence to know he was *not* saying that. No translation could ever come close to that goal. So if that is not what this verse is saying, then what does it mean?

First, let us consider the words *jot* and *tittle*. If you look at the Greek text of this verse, you will find that the words *jot* and *tittle* are not there! In fact, they are not anywhere in the entire Bible. These terms were introduced by the translators of early English versions, like the Tyndale Translation and the KJV. The Greek words used here are *iōta* and *keraia*.[22] The *iōta* is the smallest letter of the Greek alphabet, and *keraia* is a word meaning "short mark" or "part of a letter."[23]

Because the words *jot* and *tittle* (or *iōta* and *keraia*) represent the "letters" and "pen strokes" of the written Law, any attempt to apply this verse directly to translation is problematic; no English translation retains the original Hebrew or Greek letters. That means every translation has eliminated all the jots and tittles. The only way to retain them is to refuse to translate.

In order to correctly understand Matthew 5:18, the main question we need to ask is, "Was Jesus speaking literally or figuratively?" The first clue is in the fact that Matthew used the Greek word *iōta*, a word we use figuratively in English. It would make perfect sense to us to say, "not one *iōta* of the Law will pass away." In English, that could mean even the smallest and least significant requirement of the Law will not end. There are two reasons why I believe Jesus meant this.

First, if Jesus' focus was on the actual letters and pen strokes represented by the words *jot* and *tittle*, then Matthew's use of the word *iōta* could sound a bit odd—as if this verse were saying, "not one Greek *iōta* will pass away from the Hebrew Law." Obviously, there are no Greek *iōtas* in the Hebrew Law, because the Law was written in Hebrew.

Grudem, Vern Sheridan Poythress, Leland Ryken and Bruce Winter, *Translating Truth: The Case for Essentially Literal Bible Translation* (Wheaton, IL: Crossway, 2005), pp. 28-29.

[22]The reading is the same in both the Textus Receptus and the Critical Text.

[23]Johannes P. Louw and Eugene A. Nida, eds., *Greek-English Lexicon of the New Testament based on Semantic Domains* (New York: United Bible Societies, 1988), item 33.37.

Second, we need to keep the context in mind. I believe the reason some people have misunderstood this verse is they have taken it out of context. The context seems to indicate that Jesus was speaking figuratively. After Jesus mentioned the "jot" and "tittle" in Matthew 5:18, he immediately clarified what he meant in his next breath. Matthew 5:19 (esv) says this: "Therefore whoever relaxes *one of the least of these commandments* and teaches others to do the same will be called least in the kingdom of heaven."

Jesus' point was that even the smallest or seemingly least significant requirement of the Law will not pass away. Quoting Matthew 5:18, which speaks of the jot and tittle without verse 19, which speaks of "one of the least of these commandments," is one reason this verse is often misinterpreted.

When we keep Matthew 5:18 within its context, I do not see how it can possibly be saying that our translations need to reflect the tiniest details of the original form. If that is the standard, then no translation, in English or any other language, can rightly be called the Word of God. In every version— even the most literal ones—there are thousands of changes that amount to much more than dropping a jot or a tittle. If Matthew 5:18 stands as an indictment against any English version, it stands as an indictment against every English version.

The Steadfast Reliability of God's Word

In this chapter, we have considered some of the changes made by Paul, Matthew, Jesus and others. But the fact that they altered certain passages should not shake our confidence in God's Word. Instead, it should strengthen it. God is fully able to preserve the faithfulness and accuracy of his Word even though the form is sometimes changed. Our confidence in the Scriptures must not rest in total consistency of form, because it does not exist. We have seen this on more than one plane.

- First, we saw that no English Bible version has ever come close to consistently reflecting the forms of the original (chapters 2 through 6).

- Second, we saw it is even more difficult to reflect the original forms in many other languages around the world than it is in English because most of those languages are not related to *koine* Greek (chapter 7).

- Third, even within Scripture, the New Testament writers and speakers sometimes changed the forms when they translated from one language to another (chapter 8).

Despite these realities, God's Word still stands as our firm foundation. In the next chapter, we will examine this foundation more closely as we look into the deeper significance of what it means to translate God's Word faithfully and accurately.

9

THE PURSUIT OF
FAITHFULNESS

IN THE EYE OF THE BEHOLDER

*They read the book of the law of God,
translating and giving the meaning so that the people
could understand what was read.*

NEHEMIAH 8:8 (HCSB)

A NOBLE QUEST

In the latter part of the nineteenth century, a lay theologian named Robert Young set out to translate what he believed would be the most faithful and accurate English translation ever produced—known today as *Young's Literal Translation*. He was driven by a sincere zeal to preserve the integrity of God's Word in English. Young was fully committed to matching the area of meaning of each Greek and Hebrew word rather than translating the specific meaning in each context.[1] The result was a very highly word-focused translation.[2]

When Robert Young approached a passage of Scripture to translate it into English, he did not start out by asking, "What does this passage mean?" Instead, he would first look at each individual Hebrew or Greek word and ask,

---

[1] See chap. 4, "Finding the 'Default' Rendering" and "How Do You Translate a Word?"
[2] Cf. Gordon D. Fee and Mark L. Strauss, *How to Choose a Translation for All Its Worth* (Grand Rapids: Zondervan, 2007), pp. 35-36.

"What English word has the greatest amount of overlap with this Hebrew or Greek word in all contexts?" That English word would then become his default term for translating that Hebrew or Greek word throughout the translation. Young's ultimate goal was to produce true word-for-word equivalence between English and the original texts. He believed that faithfulness and accuracy in translation could be achieved only by striving to come as close as possible to matching each Hebrew or Greek word with a single English word.

If Young had fully accomplished his goal, we could look at any word of any verse in *Young's Literal Translation* and know what Hebrew or Greek word was used in that context, as each word in the original would only have one English counterpart. But he was not able to reach his goal with complete consistency. In the case of the Greek word *logos*, for example, he was only able to achieve 86 percent consistency.[3] Even though Young fell far short of his goals, that did not stop him from criticizing other translators who did not aim for the same high degree of literalness that he aimed for.

LAX RENDERINGS?

In chapter 6, we looked at some lists of Hebrew words that the KJV translated many different ways.[4] For example, the word *nātan* ("to give") was translated sixty-seven different ways, plus seventeen idiomatic renderings for a total of eighty-four different renderings.[5] Those lists were compiled by Robert Young, who included them in the preface to his *Literal Translation of the Bible*. The reason he compiled them was to prove that the King James translators did not try hard enough to find one English word for each Hebrew or Greek word. He felt that the KJV was far too free in its renderings. He listed these Hebrew examples under the heading "Lax Renderings of King James' Revisers."[6]

In the following quote from Young's preface, he contrasted his own translation strategy with that of the KJV:

> Every effort has been made [in my translation] to secure a comparative degree of uniformity in rendering the original words and phrases. Thus, for example, the Hebrew verb *nathan*, which is rendered by King James' trans-

---

[3]See chap. 4, figure 4.7.
[4]See chap. 6, tables 6.1 through 6.4.
[5]See chap. 6, table 6.2. From: Young, *Literal Translation of the Holy Bible*, 3rd ed. (1898).
[6]Another section heading in Young's preface is "Confused Renderings of King James' Revisers."

lators in *sixty-seven* different ways (see in the subsequent page, entitled 'Lax Renderings,') has been restricted and reduced [in Young's Literal Translation] to *ten*, and so with many others. It is the Translator's ever-growing conviction, that even this smaller number may be reduced still further.[7]

In a nutshell, this quote describes Young's view of faithful and accurate translation. He believed that true faithfulness and accuracy meant using as few English words as possible to translate each Hebrew or Greek word. He based his strategy on two ideals:

1. In translating any particular Hebrew or Greek word, he would use his default term in as many contexts as he possibly could.

2. In cases where he was forced to abandon the default term, he would try to boil the other renderings down to the fewest number possible.

For example, when Young translated the Greek word *logos*, he used the default term "word" 285 out of 330 times; but in the other 45 occurrences, he was forced by the context to settle for other renderings. In those 45 cases, he used 11 different words to translate *logos*.

The King James translators, however, were much more willing to allow each context to dictate how they would translate *logos*. The following chart (table 9.1) gives a comparison of the way *logos* was handled in the YLT and the KJV.

Table 9.1

	Logos Translated as "Word"	*Logos* Translated Other Ways	Number of Other Renderings
YLT	285 times (86%)	45 times (14%)	11 words
KJV	218 times (66%)	112 times (34%)	23 words

In Young's day, the KJV was the most widely accepted English Bible for use in church and at home. For that reason, in the first edition of his translation, Young opened his preface with the following conciliatory remark: "The work, in its present form [YLT], is not to be considered as intended to come into competition with the *ordinary* use of the commonly received English Version of the Holy Scriptures [i.e., KJV]."[8]

---

[7]Young, *Literal Translation of the Bible* (1862), preface (emphasis in the original; bracketed material added).
[8]Ibid. (italics in the original).

However, by the time he released his revised edition, twenty-five years later, some of his comments about the KJV grew much more stinging. This is what Young had to say about the King James translators' view of verbal inspiration:

> In such a version as the one commonly in use in this country [i.e., the KJV], there are scarcely *two consecutive verses* where there is not some departure from the original such as those indicated, and where these variations may be counted by *tens of thousands*, as admitted on all hands, it is difficult to see how verbal inspiration can be of the least practical use to those who depend upon that version alone.[9]

In another comment aimed specifically at the kinds of adjustments made by the King James translators, Young raised his criticism to another level.

> If a translation gives a *present tense* when the original gives a *past*, or a *past* when it has a *present*; a *perfect* for a *future*, or a *future* for a *perfect*; an *a* for a *the*, or a *the* for an *a*; an *imperative* for a *subjunctive*, or a *subjunctive* for an *imperative*; a *verb* for a *noun*, or a *noun* for a *verb*, it is clear that verbal inspiration is as much overlooked as if it had no existence. THE WORD OF GOD IS MADE VOID BY THE TRADITIONS OF MEN.[10]

I do not question Young's sincerity, but I think he carried his translation ideals to an unnecessary extreme. And I cannot agree with his conclusion that the choices of the KJV imply that verbal inspiration was overlooked "as if it had no existence."

I believe Young's view of translation was based on a very limited perspective. Obviously, he was not aware of the Babel factor that we discussed in chapter 7, as some of the translation adjustments he most passionately condemned are unavoidable in many of the languages God created. Also, when he criticized translators for changing the grammatical features of the original such as voice, he apparently had not noticed that the apostle Paul did the same in some contexts!

Young knew that many of the adjustments made by the King James translators were aimed at producing naturalness or readability in English, but he did not accept naturalness as a satisfactory reason for making those adjustments. He wrote the following comment in the context of accusing the King

---

[9] Young, *Literal Translation of the Bible*, rev. ed. (1887), preface (italics in the original).
[10] Ibid. (italics and uppercase in the original).

James translators of making "tens of thousands" of unnecessary departures from the original: "A *strictly literal* rendering may not be so pleasant to the ear as one where the *apparent sense* is chiefly aimed at, yet it is not *euphony* [pleasing, sweet-sounding language] but *truth* that ought to be sought."[11]

Young was troubled by the fact that some translators tried to "make Moses or Paul act, or speak, or reason, as if they were Englishmen of the nineteenth century."[12] He felt that these kinds of adjustments "change the translator into a paraphrast or a commentator."[13] If, for example, a translator replaced the original tense with other forms, as Young accused the kjv of doing, he concluded that "we are not translators but expounders, and that of a tame description."[14]

A Doctrine of Translation Standards

Young's criticisms of the kjv sound remarkably similar to some of the criticisms currently aimed at idiomatic Bible versions. The problem with trying to create a strict doctrine of translation standards, as Young did, is that it is difficult to consistently follow one's own standards. For example, he made the following remark about the kjv's repeated failure to translate the Greek definite article ("the"): "There are about *two thousand* instances in the New Testament where these translators [of the kjv] have thus omitted all notice of the definite article."[15] In spite of his indictment against the kjv, in the first sixteen verses of the New Testament alone (Mt 1:1-16), Young omitted the definite article forty-one times. Who is the judge of when it is acceptable to omit the definite article and when it is not?[16]

Young was rather critical of the kjv. But it seems that many of the adjustments the King James translators made are not all that different from the kinds of adjustments Young made in his own translation. The difference between the two translations lies mainly in the frequency rather than the nature of the adjustments. The same is true of many of the differences between our present-day Bible versions.

---

[11]Ibid. (italicized emphasis in the original; bracketed material added for clarity).
[12]Young, *Literal Translation of the Holy Bible* (1862).
[13]Ibid.
[14]Ibid.
[15]Young, *Literal Translation of the Holy Bible*, rev. ed. (1887; emphasis in the original).
[16]Many languages including Lamogai do not have a definite article.

Painting a Complete Picture

Young based his translation strategy on the assumption that the translator who used the fewest number of English words to translate each Hebrew and Greek word would produce the most accurate translation. But the translators of most English versions, including the ESV and NASB, did not fully buy into Young's philosophy. They frequently set aside the default rendering of each Hebrew and Greek word and used other renderings instead. Also, when they used those other renderings, they did not limit themselves to the fewest possible options, as Young did.

Many of the words and phrases in Scripture are pregnant with meaning; they are rich with subtle shades of nuance. Is there really any virtue in trying to represent each Hebrew or Greek word with the fewest possible words in English? In many cases, it could take dozens of English words or phrases to reflect the richness of meaning contained in a single Hebrew or Greek word.

A Multifaceted View

We have seen that some Bible versions give high priority to translating the area of meaning of each word, while others give greater priority to translating the specific meaning of the word in each context. True as this is, I do not believe these two strategies are mutually exclusive or mutually contradictory. Instead, they are mutually complementary—even mutually dependent. When a translator tries to be more precise on one level, such as the word level, it tends to make the translation less precise on other levels. So each translation has its strengths and limitations.

Think of it this way. Which of these three ocular instruments gives the best and truest perspective—a telescope, a microscope or a wide-angle lens? Obviously, each one is valuable in its own way, and each makes a distinct contribution toward helping us understand the world around us. A microscope does not eliminate the need for having a telescope. And a telescope does not eliminate the need for a wide-angle lens. These three instruments are not in competition with one another—vying for the position of greatest significance. Instead, they complement and balance one another. Each one increases the value of the others.

So it is with the various versions of the Bible. If we understand the translation goals of the various English versions and how they complement each other, that can help us glean the full richness of meaning God intended.

In Matthew 5:18, for example (figure 9.1), the Greek words *iōta* and *keraia* ("jot" and "tittle") have been translated several different ways in various English versions.[17] In this case, the ESV is perhaps the most transparent with its terms "iota" and "dot." The other three versions in this example (KJV, NASB and NLT) each took a slightly different approach. These four translations together give us a more complete understanding of this Greek phrase than any one of them could by itself.

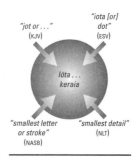

Fig. 9.1.

The KJV translators took a traditional approach, preserving the terms "jot" and "tittle" from earlier English versions.[18] (These terms could also be considered semi-transparent.)

The NASB translators took an interpretive approach. They replaced the letter *iōta* with the feature of that letter that Jesus was highlighting in this verse. They spelled out the fact that it is the "smallest letter"[19] in the Greek alphabet.

The translators of the NLT took an additional step back, basing their translation of this verse on the broader context of the passage. They chose to translate it "smallest detail" (of the Law). If it seems that there is something is missing from the NLT rendering, you are right; there is. But there is also something missing from the KJV, ESV and NASB renderings. Each is missing different components.

I believe that all four of these versions came up with excellent ways to translate this verse. But how can they all be excellent renderings when they are so different from each other? Isn't there only one faithful and accurate way to translate each word, sentence and verse of Scripture? I do not believe there is.

All four of the translations in this illustration help clarify the meaning of this verse—each from a different perspective. This blend of perspectives can work together like a microscope, a telescope and a wide-angle lens. These translations do not stand in opposition to one another. They do not contradict

---

[17]See chap. 8, "Every Jot and Title."

[18]WYCLIFFE (fourteenth century): "lettir ... titel," and TYNDALE (sixteenth century): "iott ... tytle."

[19]This interpretive rendering did not originate with the NASB. The NASB wording of this phrase closely follows the way Martin Luther translated it into German in the sixteenth century (*der kleinste Buchstabe*).

each other. None of them needs to strive for first place. Instead, they function as a team—accomplishing together what no single translation could ever accomplish on its own. Which is the best option? Is it A, B, C or D? I think it is often E, all of them: "in the multitude of counselors there is safety."[20]

Seeking the Right Balance

By now we should agree that it is not humanly possible to create a single translation that is perfectly balanced in all respects. For that reason, I recommend that every serious student of the Word have and regularly use a variety of translations—some modified literal ones and some idiomatic ones. That is the surest way to find balance in our understanding of Scripture.

Based on their ideals, the translators of each English version approached the translation task from a slightly different angle. The learner who is willing

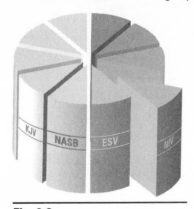

Fig. 9.2.

to walk all the way around a passage of Scripture, pausing to view it from each of these angles (figure 9.2), will come away with a more complete understanding than someone who reads and studies only one Bible version.

People often ask me, "What is your favorite Bible translation?" My response is always the same. I say, "For what verse?" I have many different translations in my library, and I consult them all from time to time. Some of them are modified literal versions; some are idiomatic. I have gained valuable insights from every one of them—even the ones I consult infrequently.

Injecting Interpretation into Scripture

One feature that sets idiomatic versions apart is that they tend to interpret more often than other versions do. But it is not only the idiomatic versions that interpret. All translation involves a certain amount of interpretation.[21]

---

[20]Prov 11:14 (NKJV).
[21]Cf. Fee and Strauss, *How to Choose a Translation*, pp. 30-31; also Daniel B. Wallace, *NET, NIV, ESV: A Brief Historical Comparison* (The Biblical Studies Foundation, 2008, www.bible.org).

When we talked about the words of Scripture in chapter 4, we saw that many of the original words have been assigned a default rendering in English. For example, the default rendering for *logos* is "word." We know that Robert Young placed an extremely high priority on using these default renderings whenever possible. His goal was to translate each Hebrew or Greek word and leave the interpretation up to the reader. That was a commendable ideal. But even Young realized that part of his job as a translator was to do a certain amount of interpreting. He knew that if he left all the interpretation up to the reader, some of the meaning of Scripture would be lost or distorted.

We saw in chapter 7 that there are many places in Scripture where every translator must make an interpretive choice.[22] For example, in Mark 5:36, there are two different ways the Greek verb *parakouō* can be interpreted: "to overhear" or "to ignore." Some versions translated it one way, and some translated it the other way (table 9.2).

Table 9.2

Mark 5:36		
NASB *overhearing* what was being spoken		
ESV *overhearing* what they said	**Overhear**	
HCSB *overheard* what was said		
ASV *not heeding* the word spoken		
NET *paying no attention* to what was said	**Ignore**	
NIV *ignoring* what they said[a]		

[a] 1984 edition.

The translators of every one of these versions were forced to choose one of these two interpretations.[23] None of them made this decision lightly. They carefully weighed the options, yet they did not all come to the same conclusion.

Another example is found in Luke 2, in the account of Jesus accompanying Mary and Joseph to Jerusalem at the age of twelve. Luke 2:49 includes the following statement:

Didn't you know that I must be $<$ in my Father's house? / about my Father's business?

---

[22] See chap. 7, "Dealing with Ambiguities."
[23] The Textus Receptus uses a different Greek verb here so in this case, the interpretive decision does not apply to versions based on that Greek text, such as the KJV, NKJV and YLT.

Which of these words is in the Greek text? Is it "house" or "business"? It is neither. The Greek wording says, "I must be in the _____ of my Father." The part of the verse that is translated "house" or "business" is left blank in Greek. Obviously, English grammar does not allow this to be left blank. So every translator of an English version is forced to make an interpretive choice. Most versions chose "house." The KJV and NKJV chose "business."

This verse highlights again the value of using more than one Bible version. Jesus very well may have intended both of these meanings when he made this statement to Mary and Joseph: "You should have known where I would be (my Father's house) and what I would be doing (my Father's business)."

SIMILAR IDEALS, DIFFERENT INTERPRETATIONS

A careful comparison of any two Bible versions will show that in many contexts, the translators did not interpret the meaning exactly the same. That does not necessarily mean those translators had differing philosophies of translation. For example, the NASB and ESV are very similar in their translation ideals. Yet there are a significant number of places where these two versions interpreted the meaning of a word or phrase very differently.[24] Here are a few examples (table 9.3).

Table 9.3

	NASB	ESV
Job 36:19	Will your **riches** keep you from distress?	Will your **cry for help** avail to keep you from distress?
Mal 2:16	I hate divorce, says the LORD	the man who does not love his wife but divorces her, says the LORD
Mk 15:44	Pilate **wondered if** He [Jesus] was dead by this time	Pilate **was surprised to hear that** he [Jesus] ... already ... died
1 Cor 2:13	**combining** spiritual thoughts **with spiritual words**	**interpreting** spiritual truths **to those who are spiritual**
Gal 1:16	to reveal His Son **in** me	to reveal His Son **to** me
2 Tim 1:12	He is able to guard what I have entrusted **to Him**	he is able to guard what ... has been entrusted **to me**

This is not a rare phenomenon by any means.[25] There are countless places in

---

[24]In some of the instances listed here, one or both of these versions referenced the alternate interpretation in a footnote. Neither version included a footnote for every one of these cases.

[25]There are many more places in Scripture where the NASB and ESV chose different interpretations. Here are a few: Neh 12:38; Ps 22:8; 119:116, 140; Prov 3:35; 6:11; 11:14; 17:20; 18:15; 23:33; 24:2; 24:34; Song 1:3; 4:12; Is 26:18; 30:18; 31:8; 32:4; 37:29; 40:27; 65:20; Jer 12:2; 48:15;

Scripture where the translators of every version were forced to make an interpretive choice. In many cases, there are apparently three possible interpretations, as indicated by the examples in table 9.4. The versions in this chart are considered to be fairly literal translations (ESV, NASB, KJV, NKJV and HCSB), yet the differences between them are striking. In some of these examples, it hardly seems like they are quoting the same verse. The different renderings in these versions are not based on differences in the original manuscripts. They are all purely a matter of interpretation on the part of the translators.

Table 9.4

		Interpretation 1		Interpretation 2		Interpretation 3
Gen 16:12	NASB	he will live **to the east of** all his brothers	HCSB	he will live at **odds with** all his brothers	NKJV	he shall dwell **in the presence** of all his brothers
Job 35.2	NASB	Do you say, "**My righteousness is more than God's?**"	ESV	Do you say, "**It is my right before God?**"	HCSB	**Do . . . you say, "I am righteous before God"?**
Job 37:6	NASB	to the downpour and the rain, "Be strong"	ESV	to the downpour, his mighty downpour	NKJV	to the gentle rain and the heavy rain of His strength
Ps 73:10	ESV	and **find no fault** in them	HCSB	and **drink in their overflowing waters**	NKJV	And **waters of a full** [cup] **are drained** by them
Prov 3:4	ESV	find favor and **good success**	HCSB	find favor and **high regard**	KJV	find favour and **good understanding**
Prov 13:11	ESV	Wealth gained **hastily**	NASB	Wealth [obtained] **by fraud**	KJV	Wealth gotten **by vanity**
Prov 14:9	NASB	Fools mock at **sin**	ESV	Fools mock at **the guilt offering**	HCSB	Fools mock at **making restitution**
Prov 20:19	NASB	do not associate with **a gossip**	ESV	do not associate with **a simple babbler**	NKJV	do not associate with one **who flatters**
Song 5:6	NASB	My **heart went out** to [him] as he **spoke**	ESV	My **soul failed** me when he **spoke**	HCSB	I was **crushed** that he had **left**[a]
Mic 6:9	NASB	Hear, O tribe. Who has appointed its time?	HCSB	Pay attention to the rod and the One who ordained it.	NKJV	Hear the rod! Who has appointed it?
Zeph 3:18	ESV	so that you will no longer suffer reproach	NASB	[The] reproach [of exile] is a burden on them	HCSB	[They will be] a tribute from you, and reproach [on her]
Zech 14:6	ESV	there shall be no light, cold, or frost	HCSB	the sunlight and moonlight will diminish	KJV	the light shall not be clear, nor dark

[a] The HCSB footnote for this verse says: "Lit *My soul went out*." See: Grudem, "Are Only *Some* Words of Scripture Breathed Out by God?," pp. 37-38, under the heading "The Lost Soul."

Lam 2:22; 3:53; Dan 4:30; 9:21; Hos 13:2; Mic 2:5; Hab 1:16; 2:1; Zech 7:12; 1 Cor 7:36; 2 Cor 11:29; Eph 1:14; Col 2:18; Heb 13:15; 1 Pet 2:6; Rev 18:3. This list is by no means exhaustive.

What is the literal, word-for-word meaning of each of these verses? No one can say for sure. All of these versions were translated by highly qualified biblical scholars, yet they often settled on very different interpretations of the meaning. These scholars are fully aware of the fact that the pursuit of faithfulness and accuracy in Bible translation is an extremely difficult process that often involves wrestling with numerous interpretive options.

In some contexts there may be four or even five possible interpretations as evidenced by the next two examples (tables 9.5 and 9.6).

Table 9.5

Job 22:29	
NASB	When **you** are cast down, you will **speak with confidence**
ESV	when **they** are humbled you say, "**It is because of pride**"
HCSB	When **others** are humiliated and you say, "**Lift [them] up**"
NKJV	When **they** cast you down, and you say, "**Exaltation [will come!]**"

Table 9.6

Habakkuk 3:9	
ESV	**calling** for many **arrows**
NASB	The **rods** of chastisement were **sworn**
HCSB	the **arrows** are ready to be used with an **oath**
NKJV	**Oaths** were **sworn** over [Your] **arrows**
KJV	according to the **oaths** of the **tribes**, even thy word

There is no clear-cut front-runner among these interpretive options. If there were, all five of these versions would have chosen the dominant interpretation and noted the other options in a footnote. The real evidence in Scripture shows that the ideal of leaving the interpretation up to the reader is often an impossible goal to attain.

How Much Interpretation Is Acceptable?

When I translated the New Testament into the Lamogai language, I had to do a lot more interpreting than English translators have to do. For example, as we saw in chapter 7, the literal phrase "steadfastness of hope"[26] was not an option in Lamogai. The only way I could translate this phrase was by choosing one of its possible interpretations:

---

[26] 1 Thess 1:3; see chap. 7, "The Genitive Construction in Greek."

- Their hope was steadfast

- Their hope caused steadfastness (in their lives)

Many English versions simply translated it "steadfastness of hope"—allowing the reader to decide how it should be interpreted. But some other versions chose to reflect one of the two interpretations, even though they did not have to. Did those translators go too far?

Perhaps the doctrine of verbal inspiration allows translators to interpret only when it is absolutely necessary. In other words, in a language like Lamogai, perhaps it is permissible to interpret a phrase like "steadfastness of hope" rather than translating it literally because there is no other option; but in English, maybe it should *not* be permissible because English translators are not forced to interpret in this case. Does that sound reasonable? Let us explore this theory.

First, would God establish different translation standards for each of the thousands of languages he created? Maybe. But even if he did, the evidence shows that every version of the Bible includes interpretation in places where it is not absolutely necessary. Consider this example (table 9.7).

Table 9.7

Daniel 11:4		
Hebrew wording *four winds of the heaven*[a]		
ESV *the four winds of heaven*		**Semi-transparent**
NIV *the four winds of heaven*		
GW *the four winds of heaven*		
VOICE *the four winds of heaven*		
NASB *four points of the compass*		**Interpretation**

[a]From NASB footnote.

In this verse, the NASB translators replaced the original words "winds of the heavens" with the interpretive phrase "points of the compass," even though the compass as a navigational tool was not invented until centuries after the book of Daniel was written.[27] The NASB's interpretation is within

---

[27]See Leland Ryken, *Understanding English Bible Translation: The Case for an Essentially Literal Approach* (Wheaton, IL: Crossway, 2009), pp. 73-74. Here Ryken states, "To be trans-

acceptable limits, but it is not absolutely necessary. Many other versions, including the ESV, NIV, GW and *The Voice Bible* (VOICE) chose to translate literally rather than interpret in this case.

Tables 9.8 through 9.12 show several more places where the NASB translators decided to interpret rather than translate the actual words. All of these interpretations have solid support, but they are not absolutely necessary, as evidenced by the more literal renderings in the ESV, NIV and NLT.[28]

Table 9.8

	Original Wording[a]	Semi-transparent Rendering		Interpretation
		ESV	NIV	NASB
2 Sam 17:16	*the king . . . will be **swallowed up***	the king . . . will be **swallowed up**	the king . . . will be **swallowed up**	the king . . . will be **destroyed**
Job 24:20	***womb** shall forget*	The **womb** forgets	The **womb** forgets	A **mother** will forget
Job 33:29	*twice, three times*	twice, three times	twice, even three times	oftentimes
Ps 2:12	***Kiss** the Son*	**Kiss** the Son	**Kiss** the Son	**Do homage** to the Son[b]
Eccles 11:6	*this or that*	this or that	this or that	morning or evening
Is 3:16	*outstretched necks*	outstretched necks	outstretched necks	heads held high
Is 8:11	*strength of the **hand***	strong **hand**	strong **hand**	mighty **power**[c]
Is 13:5	*from end of heaven*	from the end of the heavens	from the ends of the heavens	from the farthest horizons
Is 27:9	*all the **fruit***	the full **fruit**	the full **fruit**	the full **price**
Mt 11:3[d]	*are you the **Coming** One?*	Are you the one who is **to come**?	Are you the one who was **to come**?	Are you the **Expected** One?
Mt 18:15	*between you and him alone*	between you and him alone	Just between the two of you	in private
Phil 3:2	*the **mutilation***	those who **mutilate** the flesh	those **mutilators** of the flesh	the false circumcision

[a] The original wording for the examples in tables 9.8 through 9.11 is based on footnotes in the NASB.
[b] See Grudem, "Are Only *Some* Words of Scripture Breathed Out by God?" pp. 43-44, under the heading "The Lost Kiss."
[c] Ibid., pp. 35-37, under the heading "The Missing Hands."
[d] Also Lk 7:19, 20.

parent to the original text means preserving all signposts to the ancient world of biblical writers, as opposed to finding [modern] equivalents."
[28] These charts are by no means exhaustive.

Table 9.9

	Original Wording	Semi-transparent Rendering		Interpretation
		NIV	NLT	NASB
Job 34:26	*in the place of the ones **seeing***	where everyone can **see** them	openly for all to **see**	in a public place
Job 41:15	*rows of shields*	rows of shields	rows of shields	strong scales
Ps 68:9	*weary*	weary	weary	parched
Eccles 3:11	*He has made everything **beautiful** in its time*	He has made everything **beautiful** in its time	God has made everything **beautiful** for its own time	He has made everything **appropriate** in its time
Eccles 5:6	*do not let your **mouth** cause you to sin*	do not let your **mouth** lead you into sin	don't let your **mouth** make you sin	do not let your **speech** cause you to sin
Is 19:8	*cast a **hook***	cast **hooks**	cast **hooks**	cast a **line**
Dan 8:21	*the **king** of Greece*	the **king** of Greece	the **king** of Greece	the **kingdom** of Greece
Hab 1:4	*the law is **numbed***	the law is **paralyzed**	the law has become **paralyzed**	the law is **ignored**
Hag 2:4	*be **strong***	be **strong**	be **strong**	take **courage**
Mk 1:6	*He was **eating** locusts and wild honey*	he **ate** locusts and wild honey	he **ate** locusts and wild honey	his **diet was** locusts and wild honey
Lk 18:3	*do me **justice***	grant me **justice**	give me **justice**	give me **legal protection**
Col 4:18	*remember my **bonds***	Remember my **chains**	Remember my **chains**	Remember my **imprisonment**

In some cases, both the ESV and NASB replaced the original words with an interpretative restatement, even though the NIV and sometimes the NLT translated the words more literally (tables 9.10 and 9.11).

Obviously, in most contexts, the NIV and NLT do more interpreting than the ESV and NASB do. But all versions interpret—even the most literal ones. The fact that these literal versions chose to interpret when it was not "absolutely necessary" suggests, at least in these contexts, that the translators believe the practice of interpreting rather than translating literally does not violate the pursuit of faithfulness in translation.

Table 9.10

		Semi-transparent	Interpretation	
	Original Wording	NIV	ESV	NASB
2 Sam 18:14	*I will not **tarry** thus*	I'm not going to **wait** like this	I will not **waste time** like this	I will not **waste time** here
Job 17:13	*I **spread out** my bed*	I **spread out** my bed	I **make** my bed	I **make** my bed
Prov 19:1	*perverse in his **lips***	whose **lips** are perverse	crooked in **speech**	perverse in **speech**
Lam 2:3	*every **horn** of Israel*	every **horn** of Israel	all the **might** of Israel	all the **strength** of Israel
Lam 2:17	*the **horn** of your foes*	the **horn** of your foes	the **might** of your foes	the **might** of your adversaries
Nahum 3:7	*will **flee** from you*	will **flee** from you	will **shrink** from you	will **shrink** from you

Table 9.11

		Semi-transparent Rendering		Interpretation	
	Original Wording	NIV	NLT	ESV	NASB
Ps 44:14	*a **shaking** of the **head***	**shake** their **heads**	**shake** their **heads**	a laughingstock	a laughingstock
Ps 69:14	*those who hate me*	those who hate me	those who hate me	my enemies	my foes
Prov 14:7	***lips** of knowledge*	knowledge on his **lips**	knowledge on their **lips**	**words** of knowledge	**words** of knowledge

GENDER INTERPRETATION[29]

Before moving on, I would like to touch on one more area where translators often interpret rather than translating literally—that is gender.[30] Do faithfulness and accuracy in translation require every translator to reflect all (or

---

[29]Cf. Fee and Strauss, *How to Choose a Translation for All Its Worth*, pp. 97-108; see also D. A. Carson, *The Inclusive-Language Debate: A Plea for Realism* (Grand Rapids: Baker; Leicester: Inter-Varsity Press, 1998); Mark L. Strauss, "Current Issues in the Gender-Language Debate: A Response to Vern Poythress and Wayne Grudem," in in *The Challenge of Bible Translation*, ed. Glen G. Scorgie, Mark L. Strauss and Steven M. Voth (Grand Rapids: Zondervan, 2003), pp. 115-41.

[30]I used the word *literal* to describe renderings that match the gender of the original because that is the term literal versions often use in their footnotes to describe this kind of rendering (e.g., the NASB footnote in Gen 14:14 for the word *relative* says, "Lit *brother*").

most) of the original masculine forms, or is it acceptable to change some masculine forms to gender-neutral[31] forms? Table 9.12 is an example of masculine versus gender-neutral translation.

Table 9.12

Matthew 4:4			
ESV	**Man** *shall not live by bread alone*	Masculine Form	
HCSB	**Man** *must not live on bread alone*		
NIV	**Man** *shall not live on bread alone*		
NLT	**People** *do not live by bread alone*	Gender-Neutral	
GW	**A person** *cannot live on bread alone*		
CEV	**No one** *can live only on food*		

As we address the issue of gender in translation, we will follow the model we have used throughout this book—focusing on real translation examples rather than arguing philosophical ideals. These real examples point to two important conclusions, which correspond directly to the core conclusions we have reached in other areas of translation:

- Every English version has replaced some masculine forms with gender-neutral forms.[32]

- Some of the proposed guidelines for dealing with gender in translation are based on English grammar and do not readily apply to many of the world's languages.

Tables 9.13 through 9.16 provide a few examples of gender-neutral translation in several English versions.[33] A representation of each masculine form in the original is included in parentheses underneath the gender-neutral renderings.[34] These charts are by no means exhaustive.

---

[31] Also called gender-inclusive.

[32] Cf. Mark L. Strauss, *Distorting Scripture? The Challenge of Bible Translation and Gender Accuracy* (Downers Grove, IL: InterVarsity Press, 1998), p. 35.

[33] In some instances, the translators noted these gender-neutral adjustments in a footnote; in others they did not.

[34] Most of the masculine forms in parentheses in tables 9.13 through 9.16 are based on footnotes in the ESV, NASB, HCSB and KJV.

Table 9.13

		Gender-Neutral Renderings
ESV	Ex 2:11	Moses . . . saw an Egyptian beating a Hebrew, one of his **people**. (brothers)
	Num 1:16[a]	the chiefs of their **ancestral** tribes (fathers')
	Num 31:30	one drawn out of every fifty, of the **people** (men)
	Num 36:5	The tribe of the **people** of Joseph (sons)
	Josh 22:14	every one of them the head of **a family** (their father's house)
	Prov 6:12	A worthless **person** (man)
	Ezek 1:10	each had a **human face** (face of a man)
	Mt 12:31	every sin and blasphemy will be forgiven **people** (men)
	Rom 2:9	distress for every **human being** who does evil (soul of man)[b]
	Jas 3:8	no **human being** can tame the tongue (man)

[a] Also Num 1:47.
[b] See Grudem, "Are Only *Some* Words of Scripture Breathed Out by God?" pp. 37-38, under the heading "The Lost Soul."

Table 9.14

		Gender-Neutral Renderings
NASB	Gen 14:14	his **relative** had been taken captive (brother)
	Josh 19:51	heads of the **households** of the tribes (fathers)
	Judg 20:2	400,000 foot **soldiers** (men)
	1 Chron 7:5	Their **relatives** among all the families (brothers)
	Job 38:26	To bring rain on a land without **people** (men)
	Ps 146:3	Do not trust in . . . **mortal man** (a son of man)
	Mk 8:27	Who do **people** say that I am? (men)
	Lk 18:11	I thank You that I am not like other **people** (men)

Table 9.15

		Gender-Neutral Renderings	
HCSB	Gen 13:8	let's not have quarreling . . . since we are **relatives** (brothers)	
	Ps 78:25	**People** ate the bread of angels (man)	
	Num 31:26	the **family leaders** of the community (heads of fathers)	
	Judg 2:10	That whole generation was also gathered to their **ancestors** (fathers)	
	2 Kings 21:22	He abandoned the Lord God of his **ancestors** (fathers)	
	1 Chron 5:13	Their **relatives** according to their **ancestral** houses (brothers) (fathers')	
	1 Chron 12:29	From the **Benjaminites**, the **relatives** of Saul (sons of Benjamin) (brothers)	
	Job 35:8	your righteousness [affects another] **human being** (son of man)	
	Is 37:12	the gods of the nations that my **predecessors** destroyed (fathers)	
	Acts 28:14	There we found **believers** and were invited to stay (brothers)	
	Acts 28:15	Now the **believers** from there had heard the news about us (brothers)	
	Eph 3:5	made known to **people** (the sons of men)	
	Eph 4:8	he gave gifts to **people** (men)	

Table 9.16

		Gender-Neutral Renderings	
KJV	Prov 6:12	A naughty **person** (man)	
	Ezek 44:25	they shall come at no dead **person** to defile themselves (man)	
	1 Chron 12:29	the **kindred** of Saul (brothers)	

In some cases, the ESV, NASB or HCSB opted for a gender-neutral rendering even though the more idiomatic NIV chose to reflect the original masculine form. Table 9.17 provides a few examples.

Table 9.17

		Masculine Form		Gender Neutral
Mt 19:26[a]	NIV	with **man** this is impossible	NASB	with **people** this is impossible
Lk 12:14	NIV	**Man**, who appointed me a judge or an arbiter between you?	HCSB	**Friend** . . . who appointed Me a judge or arbitrator over you?
Deut 4:28	NIV	**man**-made gods[b]	ESV	gods . . . the work of **human** hands
Judg 8:10	NIV	a hundred and twenty thousand **swordsmen**[c]	HCSB	120,000 **warriors**[d]
1 Chron 7:9[e]	NIV	20,200 **fighting men**[f]	HCSB	20,200 **warriors**
			ESV	**mighty warriors** . . . 20,200[g]

[a] Also Mk 10:27.

[b] The HCSB rendering of this phrase is the same as the NIV (2011): "man-made gods."

[c] The NASB rendering of this phrase is the same as the NIV (2011): "swordsmen."

[d] The HCSB footnote for this verse says, "Lit *men who drew the sword*." See Grudem, "Are Only *Some* Words of Scripture Breathed Out by God?" pp. 31-33, under the heading "The Missing Sword."

[e] See also 1 Chron 7:2, 5, 7, 11.

[f] The word used here is *not* one of the common Old Testament words for "men." It is the masculine Hebrew word *gibbôr*, which the *Theological Wordbook of the Old Testament*, ed. R. Laird Harris (Chicago: Moody Press, 1980) defines as "mighty man." *Brown-Driver-Briggs Hebrew and English Lexicon* (Peabody, MA: Hendrickson, 1996) defines it as "strong man, brave man, mighty man."

[g] See Wayne Grudem with Jerry Thacker, *Why Is My Choice of a Bible Translation So Important?* (Louisville, KY: The Council on Biblical Manhood and Womanhood, 2005), p. 64, under the heading "The Hebrew Nouns *gibbor* and *gibborim*."

Clearly, the NIV uses more gender-neutral renderings than the ESV, HCSB or NASB. But the examples in tables 9.13 through 9.17 show, at least in these cases, the translators of these versions determined that replacing a masculine term with a gender-neutral term (even though it is not absolutely necessary) does not compromise the principles of faithfulness and accuracy in translation.

When we focus our attention on real translational renderings rather than philosophical ideals, it is evident that there is much variation and inconsistency in the way some popular versions have handled gender. In some passages, the NASB used a gender-neutral rendering when the ESV and HCSB did not. In other places, the ESV or HCSB used a gender-neutral rendering when the others did not. All these translations fluctuate from passage to passage and verse to verse—sometimes adhering to the ideals they set for themselves, sometimes not. For example, the HCSB frequently fluctuates between the phrase "God of our fathers"[35] and "God of our ancestors."[36] Consider the contrast between the two verses below (table 9.18). The Hebrew wording of the phrase in focus is the same in both verses (*'ĕlōhê 'ăbōtênû*).

Table 9.18

Holman Christian Standard Bible (HCSB)		
Deut 26:7	*we called out to the LORD, the **God of our fathers***	**Masculine Form**[a]
2 Chron 20:6	*He said: LORD **God of our ancestors***	**Gender Neutral**[b]

[a] The HCSB uses the masculine form "fathers" in the following verses: Ex 3:6, 13, 15, 16; 4:5; Deut 1:11, 21; 4:1; 6:3; 12:1; 26:7; 27:3; 29:25; Josh 18:3; Judg 2:12; Ezra 7:27; 8:28; 10:11; Acts 3:13; 5:30; 22:14.
[b] The HCSB uses the gender-neutral form "ancestors" in the following verses: 2 Kings 21:22; 1 Chron 5:25; 12:17; 29:18, 20; 2 Chron 7:22; 11:16; 13:12, 18; 14:4; 15:12; 19:4; 20:6, 33; 21:10; 24:18, 24; 28:6, 9, 25; 29:5; 30:7, 19, 22; 33:12; 34:32, 33; 36:15; Dan 2:23.

Consider also the following two verses in the ESV (table 9.19). The ESV translators chose to reflect the masculine term "man" in Revelation 4, but they used the gender-neutral term "human" in Ezekiel 1, even though, as John MacArthur states, the two passages "are obviously both referring to the same supernatural and indescribable beings."[37]

Table 9.19

English Standard Version (ESV)		
Rev 4:7	*with the **face of a man***	**Masculine Form**
Ezek 1:10	*each had a **human face***[a]	**Gender Neutral**

[a] Also Ezek 1:5, 8, 26; 10:8, 14, 21.

The issue of gender in translation is not as cut and dried as it has sometimes been portrayed. Often it comes down to little more than a judgment call on the part of the translators. Therefore, we need to be as objective as possible in approaching this issue. Otherwise, one might be tempted to gerrymander the boundaries of what is considered acceptable to include only the kinds of gender-neutral substitutions that have long been commonplace in versions that identify themselves as literal.

---

[35] Also "*my, your, their* fathers."
[36] Also "*your, his, their* ancestors."
[37] John MacArthur Jr., *The MacArthur Study Bible* (Nashville: Word, 1997), Rev. 4:6, note.

TRANSLATING GENDER IN OTHER LANGUAGES

Many of the issues surrounding gender in translation change significantly when we move from one language to another. For example, some
have suggested that translators should aim for a literal rendering of every
masculine third-person singular pronoun in the original (he/him/his/
himself). That is a problem for a language like Lamogai which has neither
masculine nor feminine pronouns. Every Lamogai pronoun is inherently
gender-neutral. Table 9.20 lists all of the Lamogai third-person singular
pronouns with their English equivalents.

Table 9.20

Lamogai	English
ye	he, she, it
-e	him, her, it
ilo	his, her(s), its[a]
ino	

[a] The pronouns *ilo* and *ino* are identical in meaning; one is
used with one class of Lamogai nouns and the other is used
with a different class.

Even though English does have some masculine and feminine pronouns, it is worth noting here that English pronouns do not function the
same as Hebrew or Greek pronouns. The only place English uses masculine and feminine pronouns is in the singular forms: he/she, him/her,
his/hers, and himself/herself. Every plural pronoun in English is gender-
neutral. Hebrew and Greek, however, have masculine and feminine pronouns in the plural forms as well—for example, they (masc.) and they
(fem.). Interestingly, the debate about translating masculine pronouns
seems to be limited exclusively to the singular—as if the only distinc-
tions that matter are the ones that exist in English. I believe this is another example of well-meaning Christians unwittingly making English
the ultimate standard for Bible translation.

Other words at the center of the gender debate are "father," "son,"
"brother" and "man." The Lamogai words for "father" and "son" function
much the same as their English counterparts. Not so, however, with the
words for "brother" and "man."

Lamogai Siblings

Lamogai does not have a masculine word for "brother," nor does it have a feminine word for "sister." The Lamogai terms for siblings are all gender-neutral—denoting either same-sex siblings or opposite-sex siblings. Here is how it works.

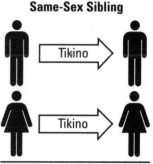

Opposite-Sex Sibling

Luku

Luku

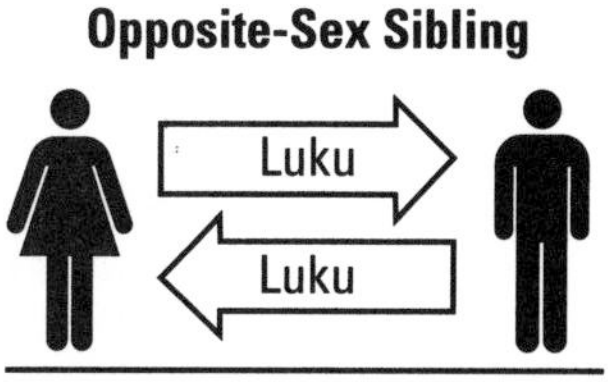

Fig. 9.3.

The term I would use to refer to my sister is *luku*, which means "opposite-sex sibling." She would use the same term to refer to me (see figure 9.3).

Same-Sex Sibling

The term I would use to refer to my brother is *tikino*, which means "same-sex sibling."[38] A woman would use this same term, *tikino*, to refer to her sister (see figure 9.4).

Tikino

Tikino

Clearly, the gender-related translation questions associated with the English word *brother* do not apply in the same way to the Lamogai language.[39]

Fig. 9.4.

Man, People or Human Beings?

Another English word that functions differently from its Lamogai equivalent is the word *man*. Two of the most common words translated "man" in our English Bibles are the Hebrew word *ʾādām* and the Greek word *anthrōpos*. It just so happens that the English word *man* functions very much the same as the biblical words *ʾādām* and *anthrōpos*. All three words can carry both of the following meanings: a singular male individual or people in general (mankind, humanity).

In Lamogai however, there is no single word that carries both of these meanings. Lamogai has one word for people in general (*oduk*) and a different word for a singular male individual (*tou*) (see table 9.21). This some-

---

[38]The word *tikino* means "younger same-sex sibling." There is a different word for "older same-sex sibling."

[39]Lamogai speakers carry over their same-sex/opposite-sex perspective when speaking New Guinea Pidgin, the trade language of PNG. They use the Pidgin word *brata* ("brother") to mean same-sex sibling (man-to-man or woman-to-woman), and they use the Pidgin word *susa* ("sister") to mean opposite-sex sibling (man-to-woman or woman-to-man).

times forced us to make an interpretive choice when translating *'ādām* and *anthrōpos* into Lamogai.

Table 9.21

	People in General (Mankind, Humanity)	Singular Male Individual
LAMOGAI	*oduk*	*tou*
ENGLISH	*man*	
HEBREW	*'ādām*	
GREEK	*anthropos*	

Son of Man

One phrase that often requires an interpretive choice in Lamogai is the phrase "son of man." "Son of man" in our English Old Testament represents the Hebrew term *ben-'ādām*. Modified literal versions such as the ESV and NASB, and also the more mediating HCSB,[40] have generally translated *ben-'ādām* as "son of man"—but not always. There are a number of cases where they decided to use alternate (sometimes gender-neutral) renderings. Here are a few examples (table 9.22).

Table 9.22

	"son of man" *(ben-'ādām)*	
NASB	*mortal man*	Ps 146:3
HCSB	*human being*	Job 35:8; Jer 49:18[a]
	anyone	Is 56:2
ESV	*man*	Jer 49:18[b]
KJV	*man*	Job 16:21[c]

[a] Also Jer 49:33; 50:40; 51:43.
[b] Also Jer 49:33.
[c] Also NASB and HCSB.

The translators of these fairly literal versions determined, at least in these cases, that a faithful and accurate translation of the Hebrew phrase *ben-'ādām* ("son of man") does not necessarily have to include the word *son*, and possibly not the word *man* either.

There are some contexts, however, where every modified literal English

---

[40]Cf. Fee and Strauss, *How to Choose a Translation for All Its Worth*, p. 28.

version chose to translate *ben-'ādām* as "son of man." One such place is Psalm 8:4 (NASB).

> What is man that You take thought of him,
> And the *son of man* that You care for him?

Apparently, one reason every literal English version translated *ben-'ādām* as "son of man" in Psalm 8:4 is to retain the possibility of interpreting this verse as a prophetic statement about Christ, the Son of Man. In Lamogai, however, it is not possible to produce a literal rendering of *ben-'ādām* that closely parallels the English phrase "son of man." If we determined that our translation of this phrase should explicitly include the word *son*, the likely options in Lamogai would be as follows:

- What is . . . *a man's son?*

- What is . . . *this man's son* (or *that* man's son)?

- What is . . . *people's son?*

- What is . . . *men's son* (lit: male people's son)?

In the context of Psalm 8:4, most of the above phrases would sound like nonsense in Lamogai; and none of them would accomplish the goal of including both interpretive options:

1. The specific contextual meaning in the mind of David when he wrote this psalm:

   - Mortal man/human beings
     (as the NASB and HCSB appropriately translated *ben-'ādām* elsewhere[41])

2. The prophetic meaning:

   - Christ as the Son of Man

It is fine for a team of translators to adopt a set of ideal standards for handling gender in their own translation, but I am not sure it is appropriate to insist that all versions follow the same standards. If a particular set of standards were really God's universal standards, wouldn't he have made sure that every language he created was fully capable of achieving them?

---

[41]See table 9.22.

Peering Deeper into Verbal Inspiration

Every detail of the original manuscripts was flawlessly inspired by God. This essential truth is highlighted in the following excerpt from the *Chicago Statement on Biblical Inerrancy* (figure 9.5).[42]

Chicago Statement on
Biblical Inerrancy
(Article VI.)

WE AFFRIM that the whole Scripture and all its parts, down to the very words of the original, were given by divine inspiration.

WE DENY that the inspiration of Scripture can rightly be affirmed of the whole without the parts, or of some parts but not the whole.

Fig. 9.5.

I heartily agree with these two statements although I think they may not go far enough. The phrase "down to the very words" could imply that inspiration goes "down" only as far as the word level and no further. Obviously, words are not the smallest meaningful units of language. Divine inspiration reaches below the word level to include prefixes, suffixes and every subtle nuance of the original Scriptures.[43] Every jot and tittle, every iota and pen stroke are in fact "the product of the creative breath of God."[44]

However, when English-speaking Christians discuss the topic of divine inspiration, they usually do not mention anything beneath the word level. That is because the word level is more matchable in English than any other level. If word-for-word translation is an elusive ideal, as we have concluded it is, then prefix-for-prefix or suffix-for-suffix translation is out of the question.

Our tendency to focus on the word level seems to reflect our English bias.

---

[42]The *Chicago Statement on Biblical Inerrancy* was produced by a group of evangelical leaders at an international conference in Chicago in 1978, sponsored by the International Council on Biblical Inerrancy.

[43]It could be said that the statement "down to the very words" is sufficient since it includes everything inside of those words, such as prefixes and suffixes. But by the same rationale, a statement like "down to the very sentences" should be sufficient because it would automatically include all of the words within each sentence.

[44]B. B. Warfield, *The Inspiration and Authority of the Bible* (Philadelphia: Presbyterian and Reformed, 1948), p. 133.

But the doctrine of inspiration should not be linked to what is translatable into English.[45] Many features of Hebrew and Greek are impossible to reproduce in the English language. Yet all those features are just as inspired as the original words are. Clearly, if our native tongue had been a language like Simbari (with commonly used words up to forty-six letters long),[46] there would not be nearly as much discussion about the word level.

Rather than saying the Scriptures are inspired "down to the very words," my preference would be to say something more comprehensive, like they are inspired down to the very smallest units of meaning and form. That would include everything from the highest levels of discourse all the way down to the word level and below—even the features that are impossible to translate into English. It should not bother us that no translation would be able to match all of the "smallest units of meaning and form" of the original, because no translation is able to match all of the "very words" of the original either.

Inspired Naturalness

We need to be careful to maintain a balanced view of the words of Scripture. Every translation could move deeper into the realm of literalness—trying to reflect more and more of the original words. That is the trap Robert Young slid into more than a hundred years ago. His translation still endures as a useful study tool, but it never caught on as a popular Bible version for general reading. If you want to know why, try reading a few chapters. It is hard work! When the original manuscripts were first written in Ancient Hebrew and *koine* Greek, I do not believe it was hard work for the original readers to read them.

The Old and New Testaments in their original forms were no doubt very natural and easy to read. Was the readability and naturalness of those original texts inspired by God? Of course it was. There is no aspect of the original that is not inspired. Since naturalness and readability were divinely inspired, it seems appropriate for translators to try to reflect those features in their translations too. The evidence in our English versions shows that there are many places where the translators of every English version set

---

[45]Cf. D. A. Carson, *The King James Version Debate: A Plea for Realism* (Grand Rapids: Baker Book House, 1979), p. 90. Carson states, "why a literal translation is necessarily more in keeping with the doctrine of verbal inspiration, I am quite at a loss to know."
[46]See chap. 7, "Translating Words."

aside the goal of reflecting the inspired words in order to reflect the inspired naturalness and readability of the original. That seems to indicate that the inspired words are not necessarily more inspired than the inspired naturalness of the original.

The Heart of Scripture

The Bible is God's Word! But sometimes, we may think of it as God's words or even God's grammatical constructions. Why did God give us his Word in the first place? Was it so we could dissect and analyze its linguistic complexities? I do not think so. There is a place for dissection and analysis, but God's main purpose in giving us his Word goes much deeper than that. Every student of the Word should ask, "Is my study of the Bible producing any real change in my thinking and the way I live my life?"

I am, by nature, an analytical person. I enjoy digging into the Scriptures and examining the finer details of the original texts. There is nothing wrong with that. But I need to remind myself that the Bible is much more than God's words, or God's grammatical constructions or God's pen strokes. It is God's heart!

Above all else, God wants us to know him. He wants us to recognize who he is and what he has done for us. He wants us to dig deep beneath the surface and mine the inexhaustable treasures of his heart toward you and me. When we hold the Scriptures in our hands, when we unfold its pages before our eyes, we need to remember that we are not just reading a book or studying a text. We are peering into the very heart of God.

10

THE HEART OF UNITY

EMBRACING GOD'S PRINCIPLE
OF INTERDEPENDENCE

Let us aim for harmony in the church
and try to build each other up.

ROMANS 14:19 (NLT)

I urge you, brothers and sisters,
by the name of our Lord Jesus Christ, to agree together,
to end your divisions, and to be united by the
same mind and purpose.

1 CORINTHIANS 1:10 (NET)

How good and pleasant it is
when God's people live together in unity!
. . . For there the LORD bestows his blessing.

PSALM 133:1, 3 (NIV)

The Bible makes it clear that unity among Christians is a high priority to God. I believe that is one of the reasons he wove the principle of interdependence into his master plan. As members of the body of Christ, we need each other, even though we do not always like to admit it.

In order to illustrate the principle of interdependence, God provided each of us with a perfect, tangible example—an ideal model of perpetual teamwork in action. It is a model we carry with us everywhere we go—the wonderful, miraculous human body. We can learn a lot about the value of interdependence by watching this amazing machine as it does its work.

- No part of the body ever exalts itself above another part
- No part of the body feels less important than any other part
- No part ever resents the parts that seem more prominent
- No part is ever glad about the misfortune of another part
- Every part is always available to serve all the other parts
- Every part is always willing to receive help from any other part

All the parts of body work together in perfect unity for the common good. If only we as Christians could function together as well as the parts of the human body do, we would accomplish much more for the Lord. The human body is a supreme example of constant interdependence, with no independence. First Corinthians 12:21 (NIV) says this: "The eye cannot say to the hand, 'I don't need you!' And the head cannot say to the feet, 'I don't need you!'" In the same way, one Bible version should not say to another, "I don't need you!" If we set any two English Bible versions side by side, we could easily find hundreds of instances where each version has the potential of strengthening and enhancing the other.

SIMILARITIES AND DIFFERENCES

When I compare myself with any other member of the body of Christ, I will no doubt find many differences. But I have to admit that my human tendency is to highlight the differences that make me feel superior in some way. Sometimes, we do the same thing when we compare Bible versions. We quickly point out the differences that seem to suggest our favorite version is best. But I think it would be a fairer comparison if we focused first on the similarities—before discussing any of the differences. Those similarities may make some of the differences seem less important.

Throughout this book, I have tried to avoid overemphasizing the ideals of translation. My aim has been to let the real translational renderings speak for themselves. As we looked at these real examples from Scripture, we saw that there are indeed differences between every English version, but we also saw that there are many similarities. Here are a few of the similarities we identified in previous chapters:

- Every version translates thought for thought rather than word for word in many contexts (chap. 1).

- Every version gives priority to meaning over form (chap. 2).

- Every version gives priority to the meaning of idioms and figures of speech over the actual words (chap. 2).

- Every version gives priority to the dynamics of meaning in many contexts (chap. 2).

- Every version uses many renderings that are outside of its ideal range (chap. 3).

- Every version allows the context to dictate many of its renderings (chap. 4).

- Every version steps away from the original form in order to be grammatically correct in English (chap. 5).

- Every version steps away from the form to avoid wrong meaning or zero meaning (chap. 5).

- Every version steps away from the form to add further clarity to the meaning (chap. 5).

- Every version steps away from the form to enhance naturalness in English (chap. 5).

- Every version translates some Hebrew or Greek words many different ways (chap. 6).

- Every version changes some of the original words to nouns, verbs, adjectives, adverbs or multiple-word phrases (chap. 6).

- Every version sometimes translates an assortment of different Hebrew or Greek words all the same way in English (chap. 6).

- Every version leaves some Hebrew and Greek words untranslated (chap. 6).

- Every version adds English words that do not represent any particular word in the Hebrew or Greek text (chap. 6).

- Every version changes single words into phrases, even when it is not required (chap. 6).

- Every version translates concepts in place of words in many contexts (chap. 6).

- Every version sometimes gives priority to naturalness and appropriateness over the ideal of seeking to be transparent to the original text (chap. 6).

- Every version sometimes chooses not to use a literal, transparent rendering even though one is available (chap. 6).

- Every version substitutes present-day terms in place of some biblical terms (chap. 6).

- Every version paraphrases in some contexts (chap. 6).

- Every version uses interpretation when translating ambiguities (chap. 7).

- Every version makes thousands of changes that amount to much more than dropping a "jot" or a "tittle" (chap. 8).

- Every version adds interpretation, even when it is not absolutely necessary (chap. 9).

- Every version replaces some masculine forms with gender-neutral forms (chap. 9).

- Every version often sets aside the goal of reflecting each inspired word in order to better reflect the inspired naturalness and readability of the original (chap. 9).

From this list, it looks like our English Bible versions may have more in common than some Christians realize—and this list is not exhaustive by any means! When we discuss the differences between Bible versions, we should avoid focusing on any of the translation practices included in this list, because every version uses them. Of course, some versions use them more often than others do. But the discussion cannot be about how often these practices are used by any particular version. These practices are either acceptable or unacceptable. If we make an issue out of the fact that some versions use them more often, that could be like saying, "I robbed only one bank, but that other guy robbed ten banks, so he's guilty, and I'm innocent."

MAKING A FAIR COMPARISON

Even though there are similarities beneath the surface, we know that English Bible versions are not all alike. There are plenty of differences. But when we talk about these differences, we should keep the following two points in mind:

1. We should not allow the discussion to center on the ideals of translation, because no version consistently follows its own ideals.

2. We should avoid making sweeping statements about any version. Instead, we should focus on specific ("real") renderings that we feel may be unacceptable. Often, sweeping statements are spawned in a sea of subjectivity.

I use many different Bible versions, but that does not mean I agree with every rendering in any version. I have never found a Bible version I agree with 100 percent; but at the same time, I have never found a version I disagree with 100 percent.

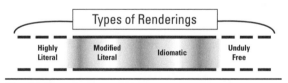

Fig. 10.1.

As we compare the various English translations of the Bible, we will find that some versions have translated certain verses in a way that may be unduly free. And some other versions may at times have stepped across the line into highly literal territory—producing zero meaning for some readers. This is where every version can help balance every other version.

It Is Not All or Nothing

Many factors have contributed to the ongoing debate about translation. I believe one important factor has been the fear that idiomatic versions would someday replace all literal versions. And since idiomatic versions do not try very hard to reflect the forms of the original, eventually those forms could be forgotten. I understand this concern, but I think we need to keep it in proper perspective. Remember: we still have reliable copies of the original manuscripts. We can and should go back to the Hebrew and Greek texts on a regular basis. The truth of the matter is that none of the literal versions could replace the original either. They are not word for word. They are not consistently transparent to the original text. They do not include the full area of meaning of each word, phrase or sentence of the original. Even so, they definitely have their place. It should be clear by now that I am not in favor of eliminating literal versions, or any other kind of version for that matter.

Many years ago, I took a course on Bible translation taught by Dr. Jacob Loewen, a recognized authority on translation. In one of his lectures, he made an interesting comment that has stuck with me to this day. He said he felt that every major language of the world, including English, should have a new literal translation and a new idiomatic translation approximately every twenty years. Dr. Loewen had an appreciation for the value that exists in both of these kinds of translations. In the past few decades, English has far surpassed the goal of having one new literal version and one new idiomatic version every twenty years.

A Sacred Trust Beyond Compare

The English-speaking world is blessed to have many excellent translations of the Scriptures. About eighty new English versions were published in the twentieth century alone.[1] No other language on earth could ever come close to matching this impressive count. At the same time, no other language will ever match the amount of controversy that exists among English-speaking Christians regarding Bible translations.

This kind of controversy would make no sense at all to the Lamogai Christian living in his remote jungle village. Which translation should he use? Well, he

---

[1]Cf. Michael D. Marlowe, www.bible-researcher.com, 2001-2013.

only has one. He is blessed beyond measure to have that one translation in his own language, because thousands of other language groups still have nothing.

The Lamogai translation of the Scriptures is not perfect. But no English translation is perfect either.[2] The difference is that in English-speaking countries, we have the huge advantage of being able to compare dozens of Bible versions side by side. In this sense, we are incredibly rich beyond the wildest dreams of most of the rest of the world. Yet sometimes, I think we squander this great wealth. Not only do we fail to take full advantage of it; we also allow it to become a source of disagreement among us.

We have been given a sacred trust beyond compare. But this trust carries with it responsibility. We are to be a light in the darkness, giving hope to the hopeless and love to the unloved. We are to offer healing to the broken-hearted and take the message of life to those who are dying. We are God's mouthpiece. We are his hands and his feet. The time is short, and there is much to be done. My prayer is that each of us will begin to grasp the significance of the awesome resource that is so readily available to us as English-speaking Christians—and that we will press forward together in our effectiveness for the Lord Jesus Christ through a living, growing sense of unity that is firmly rooted in truth.

---

[2] Cf. D. A. Carson, *The King James Version Debate: A Plea for Realism* (Grand Rapids: Baker Book House, 1979), p. 82. Carson states, "No translation is perfect."

Name and Subject Index

Scripture Index